Melanin Monologues:

A Black British Perspective

Natreema A. Adjaye

The Wordsmiths Workshop Limited

Melanin Monologues: A Black British Perspective

ISBN 978-09931834-0-9

First published in 2015 by The Wordsmiths Workshop Limited

thewordsmithsworkshoplimited@gmail.com

07931 413 751

British Library Cataloguing in Publication Data. A catalogue record for this book is available from the British Library.

The recollection of events are real life occurrences. The names of those involved have been changed to protect their identity.

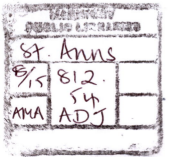

DEDICATION

To all the beautiful melanin enriched people of the world.
The struggle to find self-love and acceptance continues.
Much like the sun, the truth reveals itself every single day.
Seek and you shall find it.

Acknowledgments

In the loving memory of my great grandmother Efua Serwaa (Eno) and grandmother Ms Kate Adjei-Kyem. May your souls rest in eternal peace.

I would like to give a special thanks to my mother Nana Ohema Esther, my beloved brothers Caldeen and Rayveeyan and big sis Maleesha. I warmly embrace my extended relatives the Adjei-Kyem and Asafu-Adjaye families. To my wonderful aunties, uncles and cousins in the UK, USA and Africa (there are far too many to mention) much love to you.

I send thanks to my friends, the good ones who have stood by me (you know who you are) there aren't many of you! Ms Omiyale Jubé (Navigate Your Existence ™) and Dr Lez Henry (NUBeyond Ltd) whose kind words of encouragement gave me the push I needed to pursue this project.

To all the scholars who have committed themselves to educating the masses and imparting their knowledge of Black history, civilizations and spirituality. Your research enlightens us about our heritage.

I humbly extend my gratitude to God, my ancestors and the divine powers of the universe. I recognise and appreciate my blessings each day. There is a force beyond my own existence which supports my ability to transcend to a higher level of knowledge.

Foreword

Merely by describing yourself as Black you have started on a road towards emancipation, you have committed yourself to fight against all forces that seek to use your blackness as a stamp that marks you out as a subservient being.

Steve Biko, 1977

Table of Contents

Preface

Writing the Melanin Monologues has been a true labour of love. I was consumed with doubt and abandoned the project many steps along the way. I considered that nobody would be interested in reading what I had to say. (Unofficially) I have been composing these memoirs in my head since childhood. I have memorised the majority of experiences and encounters that specifically related to my race and on a deeper level my dark complexion. These memories came flooding back more than two decades later.

I would say this writing process was formalised after watching the documentary Dark Girls (originally broadcast on American television in 2012). I was moved by what I saw and subsequently inspired to put pen to paper.

I originally intended to make this project a collaborative effort. I hoped to incorporate contributions from various people who would have explored how melanin influenced their lives. The stories were intended to document the testimonies of people whose complexions range from the darkest shade of brown to the palest shade of white. I spent almost two years trying to find others to participate in the Melanin Monologues project without success.

I was very passionate about my goals for getting this project published. I then decided to proceed with my target alone. I felt brave enough to share my personal story and speak reflectively about my continuous struggle with the concept of my skin complexion and the way that it has shaped and continues to dictate my position as a Black woman in a western society.

I take comfort in believing that one day a person will pick up this book, more specifically someone who feels the same way I once did. They might harbour insecurities which stem from the negative feelings they possess towards their skin complexion. I have first-hand experience of this. I know that their perception of self is primarily defined by those around them. I want to give the ostracised some hope and belief in knowing that happiness is an inside job. You have to love and accept yourself before anyone else can embrace you. I know that it is hard to recognise you are valuable in a world that shows and tells you that you are worthless every day.

I was committed to completing this project because it is such an important subject. People suffer from low self-esteem based upon the treatment they face from others in reference to their skin tone.

In turn my ultimate aim is to strive to represent the change in the world that I want to see. Ideally I would like more dark skinned people to take pride in their complexion. As well as having an understanding of how blackness encompasses a legacy more important than we could ever imagine.

Take a look at society's ideas about physical appearance and beauty. European standards have greatly influenced its concept and successive outlook. In response to this universal ideology other races measure the characteristics of their own ideals of beauty against European standards.

Who would be surprised to learn that people of colour may tend to feel that we fall short because westernised principles of beauty is something that we can never attain? No matter how hard we try, regardless of the quantity of hair straightening products, bleaching creams, weave extensions or make-up that with apply to our skin. Quite frankly enough it's impossible for us to perfectly replicate those who we aspire to emulate. In turn we have to be comfortable and learn to stay in our own lane. Realistically we can only be the best version of ourselves.

As an adult I have come to terms with the fact that I fail to find people who look like me in the places that I want to be. In my youth this very disheartening. Over the years I've learnt to deal with it. Somehow it has come to be a good thing. Technically speaking I have little to no competition. There are no expectations or comparisons to be made against me. My uniqueness and individuality means that I have no one else to compete with. This allows me the space to be innovate and carve a niche for myself. I am willing to go where no other dark skinned Black woman has gone before.

I've opened up the dialogue about darker skin tones because the subject is an integral part of who I am. My melanin which determines the shade of my complexion has contoured my standard of living. Why? As I've said, there are very few profoundly dark skinned people on television or gracing the cover of the most popular magazines. Nor can they be found in influential positions in the public eye (on a global scale). Their absence means that I remain invisible. I want to bring people with very dark skin tones to the forefront of the worlds gaze. I am trying to write myself into the discourse and discussions of the latest news and into the realm of contemporary existence.

The Melanin Monologues highlights significant stages in my life where race has been the focal point of a situation or steered the outcome of an incident. The memoirs draw out specific points of my academic years because I had spent my formative years (aged five to 21) in an education based environment. The later part of the memoirs highlights other notable events I experienced as an adult.

I touch upon the work of scholars, psychiatrists, anthropologist amongst other academics and researchers. At times I have also made use of poetry to express my recollection of events.

To some extent the Melanin Monologues is a depiction of the shared reality of people who have very dark skin. I am not trying to embarrass or offend anyone. The monologues exposes my own truth in a bid to put forth an observational discussion as opposed to being critical of any other group of people/ belief systems.

I believe that the time has come for people to hear the deep dark truth.

Thank you for allowing me to share my story with you.

Natreema

———— ∝ ————

'No one can tell your story, so tell it yourself. No one can write your
story, so write it yourself'.

- Source, Unknown

Chronicles of Colour

Once I had decided that I was going to write the Melanin Monologues I knew I
needed a theme to base my work upon. I added 'A Black British Perspective'. I felt that
this would be an appropriate concept because it's an accurate description of my racial
and cultural identity.

My grandfather had migrated from Ghana to the UK in the late 1950s. Ghana
was known as the Gold Coast prior to its independence in March 1957. I was born in
Lewisham in the mid-1980s to West African parents. For those readers outside of the
United Kingdom, Lewisham is a relatively large inner city district in South-East London.
With an estimated population of 200,000 people. The area is multicultural. Lewisham
isn't particularly rich but it certainly isn't an impoverished Borough. I attended both
primary and secondary school in this community.

Whilst writing the Melanin Monologues I surfed the internet and stumbled
across footage of advertisements that were originally broadcast on British television in
the late 1980s (when I was growing up). I didn't attend nursery and spent most of the
afternoons glued to the television screen as my grandmother cleaned the house and
cooked. Watching the old footage triggered my memory. Suddenly I started to remember
many of the jingles that were played. Television was an important part of how I was
socialized. In 2013 I watch these clips back much more consciously because of my
ability to examine these images. When I was a child I had been watching more passively.
My young mind was highly receptive and absorbent which made my trip down memory
lane somewhat disturbing. I trailed through the advertisements for cars, chocolates,
shoes, toys, television programmes and coffee. I was unable to detect a single Black face
on the screen. As an impressionable child I was reading these portrayals. The world was

already demonstrating my invisibility. I modelled myself upon the men and women who I saw on TV.

During my time at school I received a great deal of negative attention because of my complexion. This had a strong impact on my self-confidence. I was in denial about this until very recently. There were some unresolved issued I had to deal with. I needed to tackle these problems before I could work towards finding a tangible solution. The Dark Girls documentary reminded me of how I felt as a child, it prompted me to reconnect with my painful past. I then asked myself a few questions. My motivation to address and answer these questions was used as a starting point to begin writing the Melanin Monologues.

Questions and Queries

- When did I become conscious of my blackness?
- What does being Black mean to me?
- Why was I alienated and ostracised because of my skin complexion?
- How and when did this inferiority complex begin?
- How did I identify the need to learn about my blackness and reconnect with it?
- Why is it important to be conscious of my blackness in a westernised society?

I started primary school aged four and completed my Masters at 21. From what I can recall race and discrimination were superficially discussed in the classroom. I learnt about it academically, more specifically the theoretical definitions. However, Melanin had not arisen as a matter to be studied, explored or discussed.

My desire to find out more meant I had to roll up my sleeves and dig a little deeper beyond the surface. There were things I often wondered about. How could it have been a coincidence that people who were a similar complexion to me were never in positions of power? Why weren't they considered to be beautiful or successful? Why was I tormented and hated? What was it about me that evoked this kind of negative response within people? As a person of colour my own value had been judged upon my skin tone, why? In my environment it seemed that the lighter your skin and straighter your hair, the better you were. Being a dark skinned person with nappy hair was the worst thing ever. Therefore I was doomed to be nothing.

In my journey of self-discovery I reached a stage in my life where I felt cheated because all the things that I thought I knew about having dark skin didn't seem to be true. Once upon a time I sincerely believed that my blackness made me unpopular and unattractive. Yet my pigment has been my greatest tool all along. I've had to review all these thoughts and feelings as well as my understanding of my identity, history, language and aspirations for my future prospects.

I needed more answers, so my journey along the Melanin mile began.

Melanin Freestyle

When I first started school
I knew I was ugly
It was when all the kids started to tease me.
My skin was too dark
And everybody was light
They laughed and compared me to the shade of midnight.

My hair was short and kinky
It wouldn't seem to grow
My lips were too thick, much like my wide nose.
I was ashamed to be Black
I didn't have any pride
The shame of it all, tore me up inside.

When I came of age I then started to see
The greatness of Black
I learnt my history.
I descended from a land that civilized the earth
I knew my Black was a gift
And no longer a curse.

Take a closer look at Black ancestry
Brothas were ruling as Kings
Sistas were regal as Queens.
STOLEN! Our thrones were left empty.
The Trans-Atlantic abduction
Destroyed our families!

The motherland became a distant memory
Slavery made us deny
Our once great ancestry.
Some were strong and kept Africa alive
There were others who crumbled
They were truly traumatized.

Without recognition of ourselves
And a fragmented history
Our culture was comprised
Because we had no legacy.
Adopting ways of life, so different from our own
Forced to take on other names
And domesticated roles.

For me I take pride
I descent from survivors
Unfortunately Black history
Has been told by some liars.

Now I see,
That Black is the definition of beauty.
I hear,
The ancestors say they're proud of me.
I know,
The power of Black intelligence.
I feel,
Uplifted with greater confidence.

The pigment in my skin,
The chemical key to life
Enriched with vitamin D
The force of solar energy.
I walk with my head high
My skin all moisturised
Like a trophy of first prize
I glistened like the sun's shine.

The truth is out there
If you seek then you shall find
That Blackness makes us divine
Because the melanised are the chosen of mankind.

BC : Before Colour

I enjoyed watching the news and afternoon television which included soap operas like The Young Doctors, Take the High Road and the game shows Going for Gold and The Krypton Factor. I immersed myself in these programmes. I imagined that I was a character embroiled in the drama or a contestant desperate to win a small fortune. Yet it hadn't occurred to me that there were hardly any Black people or people of colour featured on these shows. Back then I was still hopeful. Society had yet to contaminate or limit my perception of self. I wasn't mentally equipped to assess how I could have participated in these programmes. Dark people very rarely featured in these media spaces.

There were Black people on TV. To say otherwise wouldn't be the entire truth. At 3:30pm I could depend on Andi Peters' smile and melodic voice to brighten up the evening as he commentated in between the children's television programmes. When I tuned into Top of the Pops there were musicians of colour.

Each day I looked at myself in the mirror that was attached to the wardrobe in my sister's box room. I would just talk to my reflection. Back then I really wasn't worried about my complexion. I didn't think about being slightly overweight or the texture of my nappy hair. I knew I was Black but I'm not sure that I understood the difference between my dark skin and lighter complexions. I hated washing my hair because its porosity caused it to shrink into a tightly coiled afro each time in came into contact with the water and combing it out was painful. Nevertheless I certainly didn't think of these features as ugly.

I was safe at home. In my back yard where I ate mud pies and spent my days playing with our cat Ginger. Until my first day at school when I was released into the gauntlet of the playground. Each day I faced the challenge of rebuilding the little hope and self-esteem that was demolished by the self-hating prejudiced children who were being taught such views by their parents and guardians.

The comparisons between myself and other students began when I started to attend primary school. Some of my peers antagonised me about my African ancestry and dark skin complexion. That's when I started to measure my appearance against a Eurocentric standard of beauty. No matter how much I tried to hide in the corner of the playground or crouch inside the cupboard of the class cloakroom. There was nothing that could deter them from bullying me. Then I developed an inferiority complex about my skin. They hated me for being a Black skinned African. They despised me because of the things my skin, hair and name represented. They rejected me because of how I looked. To my peers dark skin, tough hair and broad features meant that you were ugly, impoverished and uncivilized. I know that is what they believed because they told me so every single day.

Concept of Colour

Daisy and Michael lived a few doors away from me. We played together as children. Their father was a hardworking white British man and their mother a glamourous Filipino lady who was a few years his junior. Daisy was a couple of months younger than me and her brother Mike was two years younger than both of us. Mike had a strong resemblance to his mum. You wouldn't have known that he was mixed raced. However their mother constantly declared that he looked exactly like his dad. Unfortunately this was a resemblance that only his mum was able to see. Daisy had a slightly more ambiguous look. She could have originated from anywhere in the world Asia, South America, Spain you name it. Daisy's racial background was more difficult to pin point than her brothers. We had been close friends since her family moved to our road in 1987. A year after my family and I arrived.

One evening my sister and I were at home and one of us referred to Daisy as white. At the time I remember Daisy defined herself as a white person.

'Daisy isn't exactly white' my mum corrected us. My sister and I were very confused. I really didn't understand how Daisy's skin could be as fair as a European but she wasn't white.

'Yes she is' my sister and I disagreed defensively against our mum.

'She can't be. Her mother is Filipino so she is mixed' and that was the end of the debate. We were gradually being educated about the dynamics of race. Once I was able to identify and define how race had been shaped in the wider world I had the confidence to challenge those I felt made inaccurate statements. My sister and I reminded Daisy that she was a person of mixed heritage. I wouldn't necessarily take credit for making Daisy aware and proud of her racial background but as the years went by it was nice to see her fully embrace her Asian heritage.

ACT II: The Primary School Years 1989-1996

The school environment is where I was educated about my ethnicity by default as it distinguished me from my class mates in a negative way. Before I stepped inside a classroom I hadn't socialised with many children my age. I spent the weekdays at home with my grandmother whilst my mum and stepfather worked and my sister attended primary school. In the autumn term of 1989 I struggled to find where I belonged in Reception Class. I yearned to be embraced and accepted by my peers, in a bid to make friends. The experience was all new to me and quite daunting. I had imaginary friends at home and from television shows. That was an easy thing to do because I faced no resistance or rejection back then. But in Blue Class? That was an entirely different story.

My dark skin became a heavy burden for my young shoulders to carry. A sort of social hindrance and I didn't seem to know why. I couldn't understand why I was being shoved against the wall in the playground by two boys who were more than two years older than me. They took turns in letting me know that I was a 'dirty tramp' an 'African batty clear' and that my hair was 'short and picky'.

My dark skin mattered when I was competing for the leading roles in our annual school drama productions. How could I compete with Anna and Sarah? Each time I tried I would lose and be relegated to a background supporting role. It would take years for me to land a leading role alongside these blonde haired, blued eyed beauties. Eventually I secured a part as King Pelias in Jason and the Golden Fleece this was only because there were enough leading roles to go round for the teacher's star pupils to get first pick.

Sometime in '89

I was intrigued by the music video that everyone was talking about from the playground to our living rooms. The lead single from Madonna's album that was also titled Like a Prayer had caused so much controversy when it was released. A well-known soft drinks company had deviated from their plan to support the single. Despite the withdrawal of their sponsorship deal Madonna kept the multi-million dollar fee she was paid by the soft drinks company to promote their products.

In my innocence and ignorance of youth I observed the music video where Madonna danced around in front of a wailing choir, scantily clad in a lace dress. She knelt at the feet of a big Black man. This is the first depiction of a non-white Jesus that I was exposed to. At the time I wasn't shocked by it, nor did I take the representation seriously. I knew it was portrayed to audiences for the sake of entertainment. I told myself it was only pretend. Having attended an Anglican Church and adjourning primary school I was familiar and comfortable with Michelangelo's depiction of the Saviour. I hadn't considered that Jesus may have been a person of colour. Yet I still wondered. What was so bad about this video that would cause people to think Madonna had done something wrong? However it would be many years before I would be able to contextualize the Black experience in a white space and how uncomfortable it made people (of all races) feel to worship an image of Jesus as a man of colour.

Challenging the Misconception: Spring 1991

I took my first trip to Ghana. My view of Africa was influenced by the images I had seen on British TV since infancy. The portrayal of famine, disease, impoverished people who resided in shanty towns and mud huts with straw roofs and no electricity or clean water supply. My family and I spent three and a half months in Ghana which would be my grandmothers last time in her country of birth. We hadn't anticipated that we would return four years later to the small village in Akuma Domase (Brong Ahafo district) to bury her.

16

My first visit to Ghana had restored my sense of self-worth. There were people walking the streets who looked just like me. In this environment I didn't stand out. I wasn't the only dark skinned person. Even the Prime Minister was Black. In 2013 this isn't so strange as President Obama, his wife and their children occupy the White House. But in the early 1990s the prospect of a person of colour in such an authoritative position was something that we couldn't fathom in the western world.

Kumasi (our home town) was a beautiful sight. The area had miles of green forest land. This made the region a perfect hiding place for the tribes during slavery. Some were able to conceal themselves in the dense trees. I remember how surprised I was by the size of the large bungalow style houses which were more than three times bigger than most terraced properties in Britain. The streets of Kumasi were filled with faces as Black as mine and glistening pearly white teeth. Once I had touched down on African soil I was able to see that it didn't look like the depiction of Africa I'd watch at home on TV. I don't know what would have happened to me if I hadn't made this journey aged six.

My new found sense of African pride had reprogrammed my consciousness. Upon my return to school in England I began to the challenge the bullies I would have previously ignored. I could no longer be quiet when they hurled abusive comments at me that referred to Africa as dirty, full of jungles and moronic citizens. That wasn't true and I did everything I could do to vocalise my disapproval of this misconception.

I do remember being shuttled into a special needs programme just as soon as I returned back to school from Africa. I can appreciate that three and a half months out of school could have had a detrimental effect on my studies. My teachers should have given me some kind of tests and assessments to establish whether I was lagging behind. In Ghana my mum arranged for us to have tuition lessons so we continued to be educated in Africa. Perhaps my teachers assumed that the level of teaching in Ghana wasn't sufficient enough to keep my learning standards to a level appropriate for my age. Looking back I am so grateful for going to Africa and engage with my roots.

I was given the opportunity to learn about Black African history from an African perspective. I realised that our experience as Black people had a strong legacy prior to and other than the transatlantic slave trade.

The Good, the Black & Ugly: Autumn 1991

I was always weary of Mrs Jackson. My mum didn't particularly like her either. Five years before I had been a student in orange class my mum had stormed down to the school to confront Mrs Jackson for mocking my elder sister who had the displeasure of being one of her students. This was before Mrs Jackson had come to embrace her own African ancestry.

I was too young to understand why my mum was disgusted by Mrs Jackson who had been humiliating my sister in front of the entire class. She purposely mispronounced our surname, referring to my sister as 'Asafu- AGOO-GOO' instead of Asafu-Adjaye. My mum was furious and lectured Mrs Jackson about the importance of being a positive Black role model. At the time she was the only Black teacher at the school. She was in her 40s which made her one of the eldest members of staff. After being cautioned by my mum Mrs Jackson made every effort to ensure that she pronounced my sisters name correctly. By the time I arrived as a fresh faced pupil in her class it came as no surprise that Mrs Jackson was more enthusiastic about telling me how much she loved Africa.

There was evidence to suggest that Mrs Jackson had deep rooted issues. She was one of the worst culprits for enforcing skin tone segregation amongst her pupils. She implemented this racial division, praising the white children and condemning the Blacks. In Mrs Jacksons' eyes we were always the naughty children who were ill mannered and bad tempered. Melissa was one of her favourite Black pupils. She would constantly compliment her. Melissa had 'good hair' and light skin which were the favourable traits in Mrs Jackson's oppressive class. Mrs Jackson took every opportunity to rant about African pride and her desire to be a direct descendant of an African country. I wasn't entirely convinced by her announcements. As a Jamaican woman whose ancestors were West African slaves she had the right to acknowledge her connection to the motherland.

There were many Black students at my school. But I wasn't just Black. I was a Black girl who looked stereotypically African and had an unusual surname and first name to match. There were assumptions made about me on the basis of this. None of which were positive.

My best friend at the time argued with me as she believed that I'd lied about my first name not being African. In fact the name Natreema was invented by my creative mum who was inspired by the 1970s reggae song Natty Dread. She was committed to ensuring that I would be allocated a unique name like my older sister Maleesha. A name that incorporated double e in its spelling. Natreema was born from this concept. My friend simply couldn't understand this.

'It must be African'. My mum said your name is African' Vanita hissed.

'Well my mum said she made it up' I challenged Vanita as my eyes watered, after all my mum was the author and she should have known where the name derived from. I gave up trying to convince my friend.

In the classroom each time we watched a documentary or opened a text book about Africa my heart would sink. These were saturated with images of dirty looking, malnourished children with protruding bellies, skinny arms and badly cut navels. They inhibited dry lands and occupied mud huts with straw roofs. I was so ashamed. Predictably one of my colleagues (usually one of the boys) would shout.

'That's Natreema's family' before the class roared with laughter. My close friends were loyal enough not to engage in the laughter.

I learnt that my type of Black was different from the blackness of my classmates whose parents were from the West Indies. Caribbean locations tended to depict images of a sandy beaches, clear blue skies and seas to match. These were regions frequently visited by smiling white and beautifully bronzed tourists who were pictured in brochures looking content as though they had found tropical paradise. African imagery was negative in comparison. Lifeless, neglected. What did I have to be proud of? Why would my class mates whose parents hailed from the Caribbean Islands want to be affiliated with such a negative portrayal of their ancestry? Who could blame them?.

My blackness was outlined by the imagined poverty of the entire African continent as well as the darkness of my hair, eyes and skin. My type of Black was of a lesser kind than the others. I was ugly at school. Truth be told, the kids thought I was ugly and treated me accordingly and I believed it must have been the truth. Nobody wanted to be my boyfriend. I became so confused when one particular boy kissed me unexpectedly and told my friend how much he fancied me. She shared this secret with me but begged me not to tell anybody. Of course I knew that if I chose to reveal this information then nobody would have believed me anyway. The boy in question would have vehemently denied it. The definition of being an ugly girl transformed for me when I became best friends with the prettiest girl in school.

Vanita had hazel brown almond shaped eyes and a Marilyn Monroe style beauty spot beside her top lip. She was light skinned. Vanita was the central focus of our so called friendship. Even when she was wrong, much like the incident about the origins of my name. I allowed her to be right. She wasn't particularly smart or good at sports but she was beautiful. Vanita's hair was a shade of chestnut which was usually neatly styled into three linear cornrow braids. Vanita constantly told me that she felt my hair would never grow because it was so nappy. Her hair was almost as short as mine but that didn't matter because she was light skinned and beautiful.

At lunch times we often ran along the race track in our small playground. Almost every pupil in the class chanted and cheered Vanita's name from the side lines of the racing track. The boys voices sang in unison.

'Come on sexy, come on sexy'.

The girls screamed too. They were always the first group to huddle around her despite the fact that Vanita always finished in last place. Irrespective of her loss she was shown adulation. My self-esteem was low because I knew I was unattractive. Being in Vanita's presence made it even more obvious. We couldn't have looked more different from each other. Strangely enough I wasn't jealous of her. I felt like I needed her. I was so passive I would have done anything that she asked. Luckily she didn't take advantage of me. A part of me knew she hadn't consciously realised that she had been afforded privileges on the basis of her skin complexion. She was receiving preferential treatment from Mrs Jackson who was suffering from a racial identity crisis of her very own.

There wasn't a day that went by that Mrs Jackson wouldn't talk about how pretty Vanita looked. Mrs Jackson would warn the boys that she would call their parents if they continued to leave love letters in Vanita's storage tray. She told the boys that a girl like Vanita wouldn't want the type of attention they were offering and she was right. Vanita took it all in her stride. Had she been a vain person and cared about keeping up appearances she wouldn't have socialised with a misfit like me.

When Vanita embraced me and wanted to be my friend. I had a purpose for a short while until she transferred to a new school. For the first time in my school life I had been visible because people saw me in proximity to Vanita. The boys would speak to me just to ask me questions about her. I didn't mind. At least they were being nice to me. The girls who wanted to be friends with her had to come to me first.

Looking back it's frightening to see that at the tender age of seven we enforced and complied with the games of division. The cast system of colour. The lighter skinned pupils were elevated and the darkest were side-lined. As young people we were very impressionable and had been conditioned enough and exposed to a significant amount of adult ignorance to the point that it influenced our expectations and choices. I interacted in the game, unwittingly. I believed in the colour coding system quite innocently without realising that it meant a rejection of my own self-esteem and identity. I praised a prejudice practice that relegated me to the bottom of the social rank. I was fully aware that my looks more, specifically my hair and skin were a problem. Little did I know that things were not going to get better for a long time.

Hair we go: 1992

Davika and I sat opposite one another in class practicing our hand writing. She told me some information about my hair that I thought would change my life for the better. I had come to terms with the fact that my skin was permanently dark so the prospect of changing my hair was exciting.

'Your hair can be like this' she twisted a cluster of her loosely curled, shoulder length silky ebony ringlets around her index finger. My eyes widened.

'Yeah' she nodded 'Just ask your mum to keep trying lots of different shampoos. 'Your hair can be like mine' I gazed into her hazel eyes. Davika was pretty. She had a smooth medium brown complexion. Her facial feature were unmistakably African. She had a broad nose and large eyes. Nevertheless Davika's grade of hair was good. Not kinky or tightly curled. Davika's hair was better than mine and she was aware of this. Although we were eight years old Davika already understood how people (particularly those who were Black) felt about hair. She was confident enough to make the assumption that I wanted hair like hers. Perhaps it was the fact that I was wearing ringlets that were braided into my scalp with dry, synthetic hair extensions that were a poor imitation of the beautiful hair that Davika grew naturally.

I listened attentively to her advice however I was intelligent enough to know that it would be impossible. There was a part of me that yearned for long hair with a component structure similar to European hair. Not bone straight but wavy and fine to say the least. I hoped that there was some truth in what Davika was saying.

Later that afternoon I replayed Davika's comments in my head as I sat alone in the dining hall eating my lunch and on the way home as I slumped in the backseat of a family friend's car.

Flex by Revlon, Timotei, Tesco apple shampoo, Head and Shoulders, Dark and Lovely I said to myself. I was listing the names of all the shampoos that I could remember using up until that point. I rubbed my fingertips in between the partings of my cornrows as I imagined how the transformation would take place. My hair had always felt that tough. Eventually (it may have been that very same evening) I asked my mum.

'Mummy. Davika said my hair can be like hers if I try different shampoos'. My mum looked at me as we sat beside one another on the sofa in our living room. She frowned disapprovingly. My mum had met Davika once before at a local party.

'There's Indian in her family' my mum said.

'She's Coolie Natreema' my sister yelled from across the room. Davika's Black was better than mine. Her Indian ancestry validated this. She had 'good hair' that distinguished her texture from a kinky haired full blooded African like me. Shortly after this incident I came into school with a very rugged looking hair style. My mum had cut my braids as an attempt to remove them. She had run out of time and left them in a short style so that she could complete the task of unraveling the hair when I returned from school. I was so upset that she made me go to school regardless of how much of a mess my hair looked. I knew that this would attract insults as my hair styles often did.

'Your mum can't afford hair extensions that's why your hair is so picky' Davika self-righteously shouted across the table without warning as we painted collages. I was shocked. I knew that my hair looked a mess but we hadn't argued and she had always been nice to me. I wasn't sure why she insulted me. She had the audacity to make reference to my hair. Once again Davika had taken the liberty of divulging these thoughts because she recognised and felt that her soft and wavy hair made her superior to me.

I was really aggravated by her statement. I approached my teacher and revealed what Davika said. Miss Canon gave her a warning for being nasty to me. In all fairness Davika was very apologetic and she even shed a tear. But the damage was done. She had reminded me of what I already knew. My hair was terrible on any given day.

Disrespected in Deptford

My grandmother and I were waiting in the car for what seemed like hours. She warned me to stay inside but on such a hot day I was getting restless. Grandma dozed off and I took a walk a few yards away from where my mum had parked her 1985 metallic blue Nissan Sunny. The car was still in view from where I was standing. This would have given me enough time to return to the front seat without my mum knowing that I had left it whilst she shopped along Deptford High Street. Somehow I found myself standing outside a community centre with three other children. They were most likely local kids and were without any adult supervision. I was about eight years old at the time and two of the three boys were about my age. They asked me what I was doing in the neighbourhood. Somehow that conversation took a turn for the worst. I answered the questions they directed at me hesitantly. It's likely that they suspected that I was making up the answers. They became quite irritable. I do recall being surprised that they boys started calling me racist names. I think this is the first time I had been called a Nigger to my face. I knew it was a bad word and offensive towards Black and Asian people. I remember feeling more angry than upset. When they first started saying it I didn't respond. I was smart enough to know that I was out numbered and in unknown territory. I thought it would stop because I wasn't responding. But they continued.

'If I'm a Nigger then you're white trash' I hissed unable to contain my temper.

'Nigger' the taller of the boys chanted.

'White trash' I fired back. For at least a minute we were hurling these insults back and forth at one another. The most unusual thing was that the white kid was accompanied by two mixed raced biological brothers. Would you believe that they were joining in calling me a Nigger too? I knew their behaviour was strange.

'But you're not white' I declared to the taller of the two brothers and the statement was ignored.

The situation must have escalated because an elderly Black man walking nearby intervened.

'You white' The man said to the tallest boy 'You Black!' he pointed at the shorter of the two brothers. 'You Black' the man waved his index finger at the older brother. 'And she Black' he waved at me. From the sound of his accent I assumed that he was from an Island in the West Indies, most likely Jamaica. I had no trouble knowing I was Black. The kids at school had reminded me every day. The brothers remained silent. They had enough respect not to challenge the man. Sadly it seemed the brothers had very little self-respect otherwise they would have thought more carefully about calling another person a Nigger.

'You white, you Black, you Black, she Black' the elder reiterated as he pointed his index finger at each of us. He lectured us about race but it went over my head. I was really too young to get a grasp of what he was saying. He then went on about his business and I returned to the car to be with my grandma who was still asleep. I didn't cry yet the situation laid dormant in my memory and resurfaced as I was writing these monologues more than 20 years later.

I would suggest that this incident gave me insight into how some mixed race people identified themselves. By no means am I saying that they think of Black people badly or call us Niggers. Up until this point I'd always thought of mixed race people as being Black because I knew they were not white. To my young eyes they looked more like Black people although they had lighter skin and looser curls in their hair. In the incident I refer to the brothers I felt they could identify (racially) with their white friend more so than me. To a certain degree I think their behaviour was influenced by the fact I was a stranger to them, a mysterious Black one. Their perception of self was clearly influenced by their upbringing. If the parent or guardian who was rearing them (whether they were white or Black) wasn't teaching these children that there would be certain realms of society where they would be thought of as Black (despite being mixed race) their attitude would be different. The brothers may have been more protective over the word Nigger or the use of any other derogatory terms towards Blacks. They would have understood that it related to their heritage in some shape or form.

I do wonder what has become of these boys now. The white child has most likely learnt the appropriate social codes. If he still harbours racist views he probably exercises it in the privacy of his own home or amongst friends. As for the brothers there is no doubt in my mind that their racial perception of themselves has since changed because they would have socialised in the wider world beyond Deptford, South-East London. Maybe they've been called Niggers in subsequent years since I met them. Can you imagine how confusing that would be for them?

In retrospect I'm old enough to assess the situation. I've considered that their rejection of Blackness may have stemmed from the absence of a Black parent or a positive Black role model in their lives, particularly a male one. If being Black had a close affiliation with something negative why would they want to embrace or accept it as an extension of who they were. Quite possibly they were brought up to believe that they were not Black in any capacity, which is why they couldn't see the 'Nigger' in them-selves?

We were all very young and not wise enough to understand how wider society defined who we were. Our parents, friends or family couldn't have prepared us for it. Our race wasn't necessarily defined by how we thought of ourselves. The brothers most probably realised this after being in the school system and adult working environment. I am almost certain that in these spaces there would have been times when they were labelled as people of colour and/or Black without even realising it.

The Blame Game

I spent the day with Anna in her home. We played on our pedal bikes in her spacious garden and ate a light lunch of sandwiches, crisps and fruit juice. Later in the day we played a match on her older brother's game console. It was one of the most popular fighting video games in the 1990s. Half way through the session Anna was eager to show me a trick she discovered in the graphics.

'Look' she gripped onto the joy stick with her small palms as her thumb pressed against the trigger like mechanism. The game was reset and the introductory clip was projected onto the small television screen. The rock & roll style music instrumental played in the background as we were instructed to press start in order to proceed with the game.

'See I can make the white fighter hit the Black fighter' we were looking at the opening credits and sure enough she was right. I felt a knot in my stomach. I was embarrassed.

'Can you make the Black guy hit the white guy?' I anticipated that it wasn't a fair battle. The Black opponent was not able to hit his white counterpart in the opening credits of the game. If the Black contender was going to win the duel it would take a skilled game player to help gain that victory. These were the kinds of discriminatory messages that were in our games as children, one of which subliminally educated us about inequality. Anna didn't seem to notice that there was something wrong and unjust about what we were viewing. I knew it felt wrong but I didn't really grasp what the underlying message was. I was just a kid.

Undeniably and Unapologetically Black

School heightened my racial awareness because it involuntarily prepared me for the codes and conventions enforced in wider society. I learnt how judgements were made about students and used as a basis for the expectations that teachers anticipated students would work towards as we made our transition into adulthood. My school was multi-cultural so it should have come as very little surprise that I acquired knowledge about attitudes towards race and cultural identify in that space.

During my primary schools years I was made to feel inferior about my black-ness. In turn I was exposed to the view that most things African were substantially negative, with the exception of the Ancient Egyptian Empire which we studied and celebrated. Ancient Egypt was depicted and glamorized in popular culture. Most notably in this period (early 1990s) pop legend Michael Jackson released a music video called Remember the Time. Michael, the supermodel Iman and Eddie Murphy were cast as Black Egyptian royalty. In the late 1980s comedian and actor Eddie Murphy's Coming to America was released. This film challenged the notion that Sub-Saharan African culture was uncivilized and impoverished. Sadly the country of Zamunda was fictional which to some degree made the concept of a wealthy household in the mother land seem somewhat manufactured.

Within my household the negative portrayal of Africa was constantly being challenged. I had visited my parent's country of origin (Ghana) which gave me first-hand experience of what the 'dark continent' had to offer. I recognised that Africa wasn't as dirty or poor as my colleagues believed. At school no one else had visited Africa but me. How could they challenge the credibility of my personal observations?

At the time my stepfather had purchased a mail order publication about Ancient Egypt. I kept this book beside my bed and would gaze at the photographs of the statues. In my eyes some of the faces of those Egyptian Queens' resembled West Africans and many of the Black people I had seen around South London. I noticed the similarities between the broadness of the Queens' oval shaped faces and my own. The fullness of their pursed lips and their flared nostrils of their pointed yet broad noses. The faces were adorned by dark wood, gold and bronze materials.

It hadn't registered in my mind that these figures were representations of Black people. I couldn't fully comprehend that. I could see the beauty of the depictions and for a brief moment I convinced myself that I maybe beautiful like those regal royals. My denial of the potential beauty that I possessed made me disregard the fact that I resembled the Queens. How could I? They were beautiful and I ugly, as the world constantly reminded me.

As a student I was never really taught that Egypt was a part of African culture. That point wasn't ever emphasised. There were times I would even forget that Egypt was geographically situated in the African continent. I very seldom heard any teacher or pupil say anything positive about Sub-Saharan Africa, more specifically the Black African. Nobody had educated me about the existence of Black Nubian Egyptians. I wasn't aware that the Napoleon Bonaparte and his battalion had desecrated the Ancient Egyptian Sphinx by shooting off its broad nose in a bid to eliminate the Egyptian Empire's connection with Black people. This knowledge may have changed my feelings about being Black and African. I may have had a more positive sense of self and a healthier self-esteem knowing that Black African's had contributed so much towards world history and civilizations. We weren't just beggars asking for money from the western world. As I grew up I became more aware of Africa's position and significance in the wider world.

But it took a long time for me to speak earnestly about being Black and feeling proud of it.

The rejection of my blackness stemmed from the legacy of slavery, the racial segregation of Black and Mulatto slaves. A racial division that afforded those with visibly European ancestry, lighter skin, slender features and longer hair, the privilege of preferential treatment. This was denied to those who looked more like me.

Although we were all Black there was an internal discrimination system which elevated some to an imagined higher social status. Somehow those who were deemed to be superior knew that they were being treated better than those of the lowest social ranking and that was a coping mechanism. For some people this superficial privilege was deemed better than having no privileges at all. Blacks of both light and dark complexions were stripped of their African culture. Sadly they were physical and culturally displaced as well as being far away from home in foreign lands. In the new environment they were never allowed to fully assimilate into westernised culture. They were neither here nor there. On a smaller scale we were re-enacting these scenes in our school environment. Of course we were not subject to any physical assault nor were we directly racially abused or visibly discriminated against. But the legacy of slavery, the anti-African sentiment and mentality was inherent. It is indeed a generational issue and passed down through our lineage.

Throughout my primary school years many of the Black students whose forefathers were involuntarily shipped to the West Indies and South America refused to acknowledge that Africa was part of their genetic makeup. They could proudly declare and name their extended family members who were Indian, Chinese, Native America and European. On the other hand there was never any admission or affiliation with their African roots. They couldn't see Africa as a point of reference nor could they attribute their African genetics to their Black looking characteristics of kinky hair and brown skin. Perhaps it was too painful to admit. More than likely their parents and grandparents shared the same ideology.

For a person like myself, a descendant of the Ashanti tribe. I had no choice but to claim Africa. The characteristics of this beautiful continent were evident in my skin, hair, eyes, the shape of my body and my name. If I had been born into a Caribbean or

South American family like my peers I may have denied my cultural, spiritual and genetic link to the mother land too.

The denial and rejection of African culture by my peers and many of the Black people who I saw in the media was projected onto me. Eventually it manifested itself into resentment. I perceived being and looking African to be such an undesirable thing.

I once believed that had I not been African my hair would have been beautiful, long and silky like the women I saw in hair and fashion advertisements. Or it would have been wavy and bouncy like the afro Asian girl Davika from my class.

Had I not been an African my skin would not have been so Black. Curtis from my class wouldn't have told me that I looked strange at times when I'd playfully stick out my tongue because he said it looked so pink in comparison to my 'burnt complexion'.

Ramone (his parents were of Jamaican descent and he was as dark skinned as me) would have wanted to be my boyfriend. He may have been brave enough to admit that he was attracted to me too, without fear of being ridiculed that our babies (if we had any) would be burnt to a crisp because we were both so dark. Ramone was the only Black person in my class who acknowledged that his West Indian ancestry was directly linked to his family descending from Black African slaves. Unfortunately he was conflicted. He would speak proudly about being African yet in the same breath he would make derogatory comments. Nevertheless he had no choice but to face the fact that he was African. His features and skin colour would prevent him from claiming any other ancestry. Today Ramone has three kids for a mixed raced woman. There is no doubt in my mind that one of the reasons for this was to ensure that his children don't face the same difficulties that we had as very dark skinned people. This is the reason why there are many dark skinned men and women alike who opt to choose lighter skinned partners.

I recall memories of a young Sri Lankan boy called Srihan. He was slightly older than I, but we ended up being in the same class for a short while. Srihan was mild mannered and a good student. He was always focused on his work and had very few friends. He had to be independent. I learnt how to do the same in the early years of school when nobody wanted to take me beneath their wings. Srihan adjusted to enjoying his own company as a result of finding himself in a very similar situation. In the late 1980s and early 90s there were very few Eastern or Southern Asian students in my entire school. I was familiar with the Sri Lankan community because my sister and I would converse with a Sri Lankan family who lived in a property that backed onto our terraced house.

Srihan was bullied mercilessly. I am not sure why. I can only conclude (but won't justify) that it may have been because he was one of the few people who belonged to the Asian ethnic group in our class.

The kids would chant.

'He's got lurgies. He smells like he's got lurgies'. Sometimes I would agree with them. In all honesty I never knew what lurgies meant until I looked it up in the dictionary two days ago. I had forgotten about this until I ran into Cheryl, a young Black lady who was also in our class.

'Do you remember at school when we used to say people had lurgies?' she asked 'the kids still do that now'. It seemed as though the kids that Cheryl supervised at the local school (where she worked as a classroom assistant) were not much different to how we once were. That's when I remembered poor Srihan. His clothing did linger with the rich fragrances of the spices his parents used to garnish their traditional dishes. I could detect the aroma whenever he walked past. As children of colour we should have known better than to ridicule Srihan, these were the very same spices our family would cook with.

The prejudice comments that were thrown at Srihan were from Black students. I think the school would have taken greater action if the abuse had come from white students. Black versus brown was slightly harder for them to deal with or perhaps they didn't care? I knew what was happening was wrong. I could see that Srihan was Asian but I recognised that his skin had as much colour as us Black children. I was really confused but I was used to seeing people with dark skin being ostracised or anyone else who happened to be different from the majority of pupils. Until one afternoon when Srihan was being bullied as he played on the carpet minding his own business. One of the other girls courageously protested.

'I will sit next to Srihan I don't care. It's not nice to say he has lurgies'. On that particular day I was feeling courageous too. The girl and I sat on either side of Srihan. He remained silent. These are the memories I have that make me feel a little bit of comfort.

Srihan's inability to show any gratitude for our defence may have stemmed from the fact that we came to his rescue a little too late.

My Blackness

As a British born West African my insight of race was formed by my personal experiences of being in the schooling system. Yet it wasn't taught in this environment. In addition I've examined the testimonies, documentaries and reading materials that address the history of Black communities in Britain. These perspectives represent the experience of members of African, African Caribbean, Asian and mixed raced communities. As people of colour, regardless of our parent's country of origins and ancestral lands, we have formed a shared identity and experience of racism.

For my generation our grandparents and parents voluntarily migrated to British shores from commonwealth countries at a time when many of these regions were still operating as part of European colonial rule.

They looked to Britain as the mother country. Post World War Two (1945) migration from the Commonwealth was encouraged in order to help rebuild the infrastructure of Britain. Upon their arrival to the UK Black people did not find that they were welcomed with open arms. Sadly they were oblivious to the anxiety and resentment that Black migrants would cause British people who had very little to no familiarity of living in multi-cultural environments. Unlike their white European counterparts (who settled in America) who and interacted with people of colour for many years. However Black Americans circumstances for arriving on North American soil differs in comparison to their Black British counterparts.

I rely on the testimonies of older family members and friends who provide some insight about what it was like to be a person of colour in the 'good old days'. When I was a child I enjoyed hearing these stories but I did find some to be quite bizarre. My granddad shared his memories of arriving to the UK and making attempts to rent accommodation. There were times when Black people would arrive at a property to find a sign on the door which advertised and deterred them.

No Blacks, No dogs, No Irish.

My grandfather shared his own encounters with such racist views. An Irish co-worker at a welding factory he was employed at in Manchester declared in jest.

'Gilbert you guys coming has taken the pressure of us'.

When learning about the Black experience in Britain for the generations before my own. I would be informed about how unusual it was to see a Black person on TV in the 1950s, 60s and 70s.

'Everyone in my family would run to the TV every time we saw a Black person on it' a co-worker once spoke about her memories of watching TV as a child in the 1960s. I could only assume that there weren't many occasions when her family would congregate in front of the television set. Before I enrolled to primary school I found there weren't many Black people on the daytime TV shows that I watched. I recall in the late 80s Black people were mainly in films, movies, sports and on the music channels. But Black people weren't totally invisible from entertainment.

The existing historical dialogue about Black British history (post 1945) never fails to mention the quote on quote Brixton Riots of April 1981 and the 1985 Broadwater Farm Riots. This reflects a period when tensions unfolded between the police and Black communities. Black people were frustrated by laws such as SUS (allowing the police to stop and search anyone who was deemed to be suspicious looking) for a large number of Black people this method was used to antagonise Black youths, particularly males.

In 1985 Mrs Cynthia Jarrett suffered a heart attack as the police entered her home with a key retrieved from the belongings of her son who had been arrested and taken into custody. Mrs Jarrett's subsequent death sparked outrage and was also a catalyst for the Black communities protest about local and national policing strategies. The media referred to these outbreaks as 'riots', but those who I have spoken to who lived in the communities say the term uprising is more appropriate because the people who the media said were looting, acted in response and resistance to a racist system of oppression.

Going back to 1981 it was an exceptionally volatile year. By January a fire had broken out at a house party where 13 Black youths were killed. The New Cross Fire in South East London occurred a few months prior to the Brixton riots and was deemed to be a contributory factor as tensions in the community erupted.

To this day those responsible for the fire (which was a suspected arson) have not been caught or brought to justice. This tragedy solidified the belief within the Black community that racism in Britain was rife. Many argued that this case was treated unfairly by law enforcement in their failure to thoroughly investigate the case and the dismissal of the case by the media. A fire broke at a disco in Ireland a few weeks after the New Cross fire (81). There were teenagers who also died. A message of condolence had been sent out to their families from Royal officials and then Prime Minister, Mrs Margaret Thatcher. Sadly a public announcement of condolence had not been sent to the families of the New Cross fire victims.

As a south London resident who was born a few years after this these tragic events (of 81) occurred it continues to be a topic of conversation amongst the local community. Watching the documentaries that were produced about these incidents can be daunting. I remember viewing a scene filmed in 81 that captured the crowds who were marching from south-east London to central London in order to highlight the need for the law to put more effort into investigating the New Cross Fire case. This was known as Black People's Action Day. Depending on the accounts one reads it is said that there were thousands of Black people involved in the march. In the footage the predominately Black crowd can be seen chanting the words 'racist, racist, racist' in unison as they march along Fleet Street (central London). People in the crowd were pointing up towards the tall buildings that housed Britain's infamous tabloid and broadsheet newspaper companies. The commentary for this particular documentary was provided by Black people who walked amongst the crowd that day. They recalled how they were shouting the words 'racist, racist, racist' in response to some of the journalists and employees who were standing at the windows, hurling racist abuse at them from above. I found the narrators testimony to be interesting. Without it, audiences would not have known that those who were protesting were being racially abused and insulted by those so called professionals who worked in those office buildings as part of the print media industry. The camera man didn't capture the source of abuse that was vented towards the people who protested in honour of their loved ones. I couldn't help but concluded that the cameraman's failure to pan its focus towards the office windows was intentional.

The momentous release of Nelson Mandela from prison in 1990 was the first story that I can remember seeing which had held such a strong sentiment of issues relating to racism and inequality. Unlike my grandparents and parents I hadn't been around to witness the racial tensions and struggle of Blacks in South Africa that had been documented and broadcast as these events and uprisings were unfolding in response to the racist apartheid regime.

From my memory I would regard Stephen Lawrence's murder in 1993 as particularly shocking for me. The incident took place in Eltham which is only a few miles from where I lived at the time. Nothing like that occurred so close to home for me. The Lawrence family were related to some students I went to school with in Lewisham. Until then I had only heard about racially violent crimes against people of colour. Seeing this case news and hearing people talk about it made it more of a reality to me. I then became educated about how being oblivious to one's blackness could have dangerous consequences, simply because we needed to understand it in order to protect ourselves. The word on the street back in the early 1990s was that as a Black person there were some areas in the city you knew you couldn't go because it could cost you your life. This was our reality and as a person of colour you were extremely aware of it.

In loving memory of Stephen Lawrence 1974-1993

Sometimes it's hard to believe
You left this world in '93.
The angels came and took you home,
Now you're in heaven at God's throne.

You were young and shone so bright
As you travelled home that faithful night,
How could you have known an evil force?
Would intervene and change life's course?

Without good reason you were gone,
To them they saw your skin as wrong.
For years they wouldn't tell us why,
They just denied it and told lies.

Your family fought and kept so strong,
That's why your legacy lives on.
Though you're not here, we see and feel
Your presence on this earth was real.

Brother Stephen, as you peacefully lay
We remember you as we kneel and pray.
May you rest eternally in peace,
And pray the Lord your soul to keep.

Affirmation

Being told I'm ugly
Has helped me to see
Unusual can be lovely
I can only be me.

I'm no supermodel
Yet I'm proud to be me
Like a blossoming flower
Self-assured, humbly.

If you feel strange
Embrace being different
Be unique and don't change,
Just to fit in the crowd.

Beauty exists in all forms
Depends on how you see it.
If they say you're ugly
Reject it, don't believe it.

For your difference be proud
Shout it out loud
Look in the mirror
Smile and love what you see.
You're brilliant and special
As god intended
The critics are ignorant
So please don't be offended.

A New Beginning: Autumn 1996

I was a fish out of water in secondary school. I felt intimidated by all the things that were put before me. The size of the older pupils, the workload and the building. Everything seemed so much bigger. I was way out of my depth. I had suffered from chicken pox in the summer of 96. By the time I enrolled to secondary school the scarring was healing and turning into black blemishes. I didn't want to go to school that first semester. Naturally my parents forced me to.

This was the first time I was in a same sex school environment which was proving itself to be as catty as the one I had graduated from. The students in my year group were not exactly mean to me. It was my lack of confidence that made me feel uneasy.

Adolescent years were proving to be a challenge. I was very insecure about my looks and my childlike body was transforming into that of a young woman. I was dealing with issues relating to puberty and my skin colour simultaneously.

Socialising after school was especially difficult for me. I hated going to the shopping mall where other teenagers congregated. Nine times out of ten I was verbally abused as I walked on the streets. The groups of young boys were relentless. Someone from the crowd would shout a derogatory name like 'Black Monkey' or 'Black attack'.

The adjective Black was often used as a precursor for negative words to describe my complexion. I became objectified without an identity beyond my Blackness. They didn't see me as a person with feelings. They didn't care that a few hurtful words could have a permanent and detrimental effect upon my perception of self. This was one of my lowest periods.

In secondary school I couldn't hide. I hoped to be swamped up by the size of the environment. I believed that this would be the perfect place to go unnoticed. Instead my problems were amplified. I became uglier and more afraid. I compared myself to the other girls who were slimmer, lighter skinned and had longer hair. They achieved higher grades than I did academically.

Friendship Factor: Autumn 1997

The first academic year had sped by and I was becoming more settled in my new surroundings. My two best friends were white. I didn't consciously make the effort to pick them on the basis of skin colour. I just happened to gravitate towards Vanessa and Heather. We were like the three musketeers who became inseparable.

Our daily dialogue didn't include race related matters. At aged 12 it hadn't become on obvious issue yet. Our existence was very small. The world we inhabited consisted of our classroom, our bedrooms, the playground and gossiping on the telephone. There wasn't a single reference made about colour until the three of us got into a heated argument. I was aware that Heather's dad was slightly prejudice. Quite ironically he was a dark skinned Polish man, most likely of Jewish ancestry. Heather told me that her friends at primary school had mistaken him for a mixed raced person at times when they returned from their annual holiday. His complexion was susceptible to tanning. This look manifested in Heather, she had very dark hair and an olive complexion.

After an argument that took place between the three of us (I can't remember who started it or what it was all about) Heather told me that she had been given a lift home from an event she attended with Vanessa and her family. On the journey back Vanessa's step father had stopped at a set of traffic lights. A car full of Black men had pulled up alongside them. Heather told me that a racist comment had been made by Vanessa's stepfather and the adult passengers were amused by his outburst.

I was stunned by this admission. Perhaps my ignorance of youth had made me believe that Vanessa's tolerance towards racial diversity was reflective of her family's attitudes and beliefs. Without knowing all the facts my emotions led me to confront Vanessa about the accusations. Naturally she became very defensive and upset. She was clearly embarrassed by Heather's claim. Most unfortunately the three of stopped socialising for a many months. Our friendship was permanently strained when the issue of race had been added to the dynamics of our relationship.

We were protected by our innocence and ignorance for a long time. We shared the misconstrued belief that colour didn't matter. These were the days before our perspectives of race had become influenced and somewhat corrupted by the wider world.

Understandably Vanessa denied the accusations of her father's bigoted views. Who would have admitted that? In retrospect I believe that Vanessa was in denial or oblivious to the fact that her family was prejudice. She may have become accustomed to the fact that these comments and thoughts were an ordinary part of their behaviour. Vanessa had most likely been over exposed to racism at home which could have resulted in her rejection and resilience towards acknowledging it. Vanessa may have never been confronted with need to address it beforehand. I was the first Black friend she had become close to despite the fact that she lived in Southwark. One of the most multi-cultural Boroughs in South-East London. Her family hadn't really interacted with people of colour until Vanessa and her sister Linda went to school and each of them befriended a Black girl. Vanessa and I remained on speaking terms until we graduated from secondary school. Heather went onto marry a West African man.

I gave Vanessa some insight into race. She was able to closely observe my experiences as a Black person living in Britain. I had even invited her to Ghana and she happily accepted. This proposal didn't materialise as we'd planned to take the trip after leaving school. Sadly we didn't fulfil this goal.

When we were teens I frequently visited Asian owned hair and cosmetic stores after school. They stocked products specifically designed for Afro hair. Vanessa would sometimes accompany me to the shops. She always expressed how intrigued she was by the smell and appearance of these retails stores.

'I find these shops so fascinating. How come there are so many products? What are they used for?'. She proclaimed in owe as her blue eyes scanned the multiple shelves that were filled with creams, serums and potions. All of which were labelled with a promise to transform and beautify afro hair.

Each day we walked to and from school together. On one particular occasion the subject of our conversation had reverted back to the race debate that happened at school earlier that day. I can't remember the details but I recall the concluding discussion myself and Vanessa held as we walked towards Lewisham shopping mall.

'Well you know in this world' I said as I was feeling self-righteous 'I'm going to have it a lot harder than you because I'm a Black person' my hands were waving as they often did when I wanted to emphasise an important point.

Vanessa's head lowered towards the ground as we walked in silence for a few awkward seconds.

I looked at her and she stole a quick glance at me. Her face was red. I took a deep breath as I regretted my statement just as soon as I'd uttered those words.

'No I don't believe that!' she protested 'we're all equal. Our colour doesn't matter. It shouldn't matter!' Vanessa added.

'You're right' I nodded in agreement 'Yes we're all the same' I retracted my statement in a bid to prevent causing any further offence to my friend.

Deep down inside my feelings and beliefs were quite the opposite. I'd witnessed enough situations to know that Vanessa and I shared many of the same interests. However in the context of race the scales were drastically unbalanced. There were some places and levels of success that would become inaccessible to me because of the colour of my skin as opposed to my abilities and personal character. Vanessa was unable to accept that her whiteness created an element of privilege for her in the world, particularly within European social systems. I am not entirely sure whether Vanessa's denial was conscious or subconscious. I doubt whether she really grasped the complexity of race relations at such a young age.

When I think about Vanessa's attitude towards race. I recall an incident when a girl who I'd had attended primary school with was having a conversation with Vanessa in the girl's toilets. The young lady called Celetia had told Vanessa about something that had happened between myself and Celetia. This referred to an incident that happened many years before when we were in primary school. At the time I may have been 10 years old and Celetia no more than eight. Apparently I'd told Celetia the importance of her never forgetting her African Caribbean cultural roots. Celetia was of mixed heritage, born to a white mother and a West Indian father. Her father had abandoned the family. Initially I hadn't realised that Celetia was of dual heritage because her physical appearance was much more reflective of her European ancestry. Nevertheless once Celetia enlightened me about her ethnic composition I lectured her. Even in my youth I was passionate about race and identity. That was how I'd been raised by my mum. I was taught to never forget where I'd had come from.

I can remember this conversation vaguely. I was dumbfounded by the fact that Celetia had retained the details in her mind for so many years. In the space of a decade Celetia's mother and little sister (her sister was severely disabled) had sadly died. By the time she had reached secondary school Celetia was in foster care.

Vanessa returned to the classroom at lunchtime to share Celetia's testimony of racial liberation, one of which I'd unwittingly influenced. Vanessa was visibly irritated, huffing and puffing. I thought this was because she was saddened by Celetia's present situation, having experienced so much loss in her family.

'She [Celetia] kept saying to me, you know your friend told me that, the one who's really, really dark' Vanessa hissed. 'Why did she have to say the one who's really dark? Couldn't she have just said Black?' Vanessa enquired with a frown.

'Well I'm dark Vanessa, it doesn't matter' I replied as I couldn't understand why Vanessa was so aggravated by the fact that Celetia had referred to me as a very dark skinned person. Wasn't that true?

There is something about blackness in this context that Vanessa deemed as substantially negative. I was more offended by Vanessa's reaction than Celetia's description of me. I was learning how to take pride in my blackness. Was it something I should have been ashamed of?

Cover Coloured Girls. Who's the Fairest of Them All? 1999

A prospectus was being put together to promote our school to parents and guardians who were searching for a high school for their children. The senior management team were selecting the girls who would grace the front cover and reflect the diversity of our learning environment.

The girls who were eventually selected for the final line up were very well presented. A few of them were girls of colour, but there weren't any dark skinned faces amongst those finalists. Back then I thought they were deliberately employing the same colour bias towards complexion practiced in the media. In terms of what was an acceptable kind of Black face that could be used to represent and celebrate the schools diversity. Just as long as that face wasn't too Black. Madison, a fellow colleague made an interesting comment about the situation.

'I'm too Black for them' she joked. The truth is, she was one of the brightest (if not the most intelligent student) in our year group. In comparison to my complexion Madison's skin was a milk chocolate shade. If she couldn't grace the cover of our school's prospectus with all her intelligence and a lighter complexion than mine, then I stood absolutely no chance! As teenagers we were smart enough to decode the secret criteria and preferential treatment that was being implemented by the teachers in their selection of those who were chosen to be on the cover of that brochure. They were so blatantly biased in their choice. I didn't expect to be chosen. I was never one of their golden girls. Nevertheless when Madison was excluded from the bunch I clearly understood how important colour/complexion factored into these kinds of decisions.

Sometimes I felt that it didn't matter how smart, pretty, kind or ambitions you were. Your skin colour (especially if it was dark) took precedence over anything and everything else. Skin complexion became indistinguishable from individual identify regardless of what equality and diversities policies they tried to promote and ram down our throats.

A very similar selection process was implemented when we were told that a documentary was to be filmed by one of the major British TV broadcasters at our school. The documentary may have been filmed before the prospectus but it all happened within a similar time frame. Some of the same girls were picked to be in it. Once again they had the same acceptable skin tone which validated their presence on the cover of the schools guide.

New Mel-lennium: January 2000

We had survived the new Millennium! The world didn't end on 31st December 1999 a few minutes shy of the midnight hour. The global computer systems and electronic devices didn't malfunction because of its failure to recognise the date 01/01/00. As far as the dates were concerned everything reset back to 0, the systems that failed to recognise 2000 simply reverted to 1900.

I was 15 years old with a year to go before I was sit my GCSE's exams. On the brink of graduating from secondary school this was my first conscious encounter with 'melanin' (I don't ever recall hearing it being mentioned to me before this period). The word was uttered on a school trip to the Millennium Dome (an indoor exhibition encompassed in a circular dome like building in a derelict site in Greenwich, south London). This landmark was erected in celebration of the year 2000 and has since been renovated into the 02 arena which houses a concert stadium, restaurants and a multiplex cinema.

Destiny and I were in the same year group at school. She uttered the word melanin as a young albino student from another school walked passed us. Destiny briefly explained how the student lacked pigment which caused their pale complexion although they were genetically Black. I was familiar with the term albino and I'd seen people who had this recessive gene. Destiny wasn't particularly interested in elaborating on this subject. She began to have another conversation with a fellow classmate. I kept tapping her on the shoulder as she grudgingly shared one further piece of information with me.

'The colour of our eyes' Destiny pointed to the lenses of her rectangular spectacles. Her eyes were as dark as mine yet her skin was much lighter (her mother being mixed raced and father African Caribbean).

'That's pigmentation. We've got melanin in our eyes' she added.

'Our eyes too?' I asked.

'Yes the colour in our eyes and skin is because we have melanin' Destiny stated before she walked off. She was determined not to tell me anymore. I was puzzled by the information she had divulged to my young mind. I was fascinated. Why had nobody ever mentioned melanin before? I don't remember being told anything about it in my science lessons at primary or secondary school. There wasn't any memorable information shared that was significant enough for me to recall ever hearing about it. Not a single person had explained to me the scientific difference between racial groups. At school we had studied humans' internal organs and the reproductive differences between males and females. I'd learnt about plant cells, photosynthesis, stems and so forth. But nothing about melanin. If this thing was making me Black then why didn't I know about it?

During my secondary school days learning anything more than the information that was required to pass exams didn't interest me whatsoever. However, Destiny had ignited my learning spark. It would be a number of years before I lit the flame of knowledge. I didn't think of educating myself about my blackness and African history pre- colonisation (more specifically the days before Ghana's retained its independence) or before the slave trade swept across the African continent, destabilising the economic, social and political structure of civilizations. At school I received a brief update about slavery which I think was crammed into three history lessons (it may well have been less). I never enjoyed history which maybe the reason why I chose not to study it beyond the age of 14. I found it difficult to retain information about the Cold War and the Battle of Waterloo. I couldn't recall the story of Henry VIII no matter how many times I read the text book. Subconsciously my inability to preserve this information may have been caused by my brains involuntary rejection on a spiritual level.

How could I acquire the details and history of other races when I knew so little about African history? I recall on that very same visit to the Millennium Dome there was a photo booth that could convert images of people to a different race. Heather stood at the screen and smiled as the machine processed her photo and she transformed into a Black girl. The entire class cheered in excitement as the photo booth churned and produced an image of an aboriginal looking Heather. Everyone laughed. I studied the image. With the exception of the broad nose, Heather's natural skin tone looked very similar to her Black clone. Which didn't surprise me as I always believed that her olive skin and dark hair meant she had some Jewish or Roma ancestry in her blood line.

'Natreema!' a random voice hollered 'you try it. Let's see yours'. Within seconds my entire class was demanding that I step inside the photo booth and see what the race machine would conjure up from my African self. I declined and the cries grew louder.

'Come on just try it' my friend Melanie moaned. The more I seemed to resist the more they urged me on. My disapproval was my natural instinct against taking pictures at friends party's or school. In those days I would nervously wait as the pictures were sent to the photo lab to be developed. My pictures always came out very dark. I was extremely self-conscious about this. Of course the pictures would be dark because of my skin tone. In my late teens I came to realise that the flash and lighting of these cameras were not designed to detect the skin tones of people with very dark complexions. Subsequently in my photos my skin complexion had a tendency to appear grey, green and sometimes I achieved a metallic looking finish.

That day at the Dome I had another reason for not wanting to enter the booth. The more my colleagues pressurised me into entering the booth, the more defensive I became. Their obsession was perverse. Why did they want to see what I would look like as a white person? I wasn't willing to act out their fantasy. At some point the teacher intervened on a mission to coax me into playing the race change game. I stood my ground. Shortly before this incident there was a campaign launched on British TV where celebrities engaged in the same exercise. The Spice Girl Mel B had been changed into a white woman with the help of prosthetics. I thought this was quite bizarre. I remember coming into school the following day and everybody in the class was talking about it. My colleagues were amazed by the advancement in technology, special effects and the possibility of seeing what one would look like if they belonged to a different racial group. This didn't appeal to me in the slightest bit.

Ethnic Enlightenment: Autumn 2001

As I approached the end of the compulsory school system I was being exposed to more ideas about the divisive nature of society. Classes had been separated into sets based upon the academic ability of students. These structures had a tendency to amend friendship groups because students would begin to socialise with those who were in the majority of their classes as opposed to the friends they used to hang out with for fun.

A few of us girls were growing out of our shells and blossoming in terms of wearing make-up and starting relationships with boys. We were generally getting more confident. Those who were regarded as pretty in a conventional sense knew they possessed the power to manipulate situations based upon their looks. For the first time in my life, my aspirations seemed real. I was beginning to understand that the choices I made could determine the type of job I would get as an adult. My awareness gave me a greater sense of self-assurance. I was conscious of the control I had over my own destiny.

I started caring about my appearance. I waxed my eyebrows and wore make-up (which never failed to stain my white school shirts). People actually started to call me pretty. I felt attractive but I certainly didn't believe that I was pretty or beautiful. Boys my own age never expressed any romantic interest towards me but I was no longer receiving as much verbal abuse on my way to the shopping mall. Perhaps I was starting to look a bit more normal in other people's eyes. The little male attention I did receive was from older men and that wasn't the type of accolades I wanted as it made me feel dirty. Some of those guys were older than my parents!

At the beginning of the new academic term the head teacher had arranged for professionals to visit our school. We were given the opportunity to discuss our career choices. The exam hall was filled with students, teachers and 'the professionals'. To us teenagers the professionals had reached the pinnacle of success. They were doing jobs that we dreamt of.

I went from table to table without a clear indication of the occupation that I wanted to pursue in the future. I was excited about speaking to people and getting some ideas. From that day I can only seem to remember one particular session I had with a man. Strangely enough I don't recall what his profession was. I don't think he even told me. He was white, middle aged and overweight with grey hair. This man was smartly dressed and wore black spectacles which made him look somewhat intelligent. He had the look of importance and he spoke with a posh English accent. The type of drawl that most would achieve through elocution lessons.

Just as soon as I sat down to speak with him I regretted my decision to do so. I was supposed to be asking him for career advice but it turned out to be an interrogation session. He was more interested in knowing about my past background and not my future plans.

'What do you like to read?' he stared at me.

'Erm I like World War One literature' I gave this answer as I believed that it would be the type of thing that would impress a middle class professional like himself.

'What type of literature?' I noticed that he was staring at me with such intensity he hadn't even blinked.

'Stuff about the effects of the world war. The trauma the soldiers suffered when they returned home'. I proudly exclaimed with a smile. I thought this would be enough to arouse the self-appointed detective's curiosity. He hadn't changed his facial expression which suggested that he was still waiting for me to go into detail. So I did.

'The themes are interesting as they discuss comradeship between the soldiers, bereavement, shell shock...'

'What's your favourite poem?' he interrupted before I could complete my list of likes.

'I really like hero by Sassoon' I had to think quickly.

I was quite weary of this man and he was clearly sceptical of me. I suspected that he was asking me these questions as an attempt to catch me out. He obviously didn't believe that I knew anything about world war one themed literature. The questions kept coming. I eventually ran out of answers. I do recall feeling angry with myself for allowing him to have the final world. I remained silent after 20 minutes of non-stop questions. I accepted defeat. But how could a 16 year old student compete with the knowledge of a balding middle aged man?.

The aged interrogator smirked as he removed his glasses from his sweaty nose. He was satisfied that he had disarmed a defenceless teenage girl who was seeking careers advice from him. He placed the frames on the table and lent towards me.

'Interviewers will ask you all sorts of questions. Especially if you say you like something' he said.

'You must know as much about World War One poetry as you would know about the So Solid Crew'.

My heart sank. Why on earth did this man make a comparison between my knowledge of world war poetry to a chart topping music band? The So Solid Crew were a popular group at the time but it wasn't as if I knew enough about them to write an encyclopedia on their music. This comment confirmed what I already knew about this dude. He thought that inner city Black kids like myself were only interested and knowledgeable about music and popular culture. I had witnessed many stereotypical and prejudice statements at school to know when someone was being ignorant.

With the encouragement of a fellow student (an Asian girl who always achieved A* grades) I made an appointment to see our head teacher to discuss my concerns about the man who I spoke to during the careers fair.

When we entered the head teacher's office I assumed that as a woman of colour she would automatically empathise with my encounter of subliminal prejudice. This was quite the contrary. She told us that it was unlikely that the man was trying to cause any offence. He simply wanted to show that he knew about the latest musicians in popular culture. She claimed that he was trying to look 'cool and hip'.

'He probably named the first band that he could think of' the head mistress said dismissively as she laughed. I smiled politely at her prediction but I wasn't convinced. I don't think she truly believed in what she was saying either.

To make us feel better and prove that she too could relate to racial misunderstandings she went onto recall an incident when she had made a false judgement of racism during the time she spent growing up in South Africa. She had a white best friend. Our head teacher described how she thought her friend's brother hated her because she was 'Cape Coast Coloured'. This was a racial terminology I hadn't heard of before that day. The guy she spoke of wouldn't speak to her. She explained how their paths crossed many years later and they got a chance to reflect upon their past encounters. Apparently they both realised that they had made false assumptions about one another. This man admitted that he felt uncomfortable talking to my head teacher when they were teens because he thought she resented him as a white man due to the tensions between the white and non-white communities in South Africa. I continued to smile and nod as she waffled on about racial misunderstandings and assumptions. I'd stopped listening. Mentally I'd somehow switched off to be honest.

My head teacher's denial of the man's attitude at the careers fair was as offensive as the statement he made. She acted as if my perception of being stereotyped was imagined and I was merely being overly sensitive. I knew exactly what the man at the fair was trying to imply. I couldn't understand why my head teacher failed to acknowledge it too. She had asked me his name so she was aware of exactly who I was talking about. Perhaps this man had been one of the chairs on the schools governing body and she didn't want me to make a complaint. He may have been a friend of hers? I then considered that my head teacher might have been trying to protect me by disregarding such small instances of prejudice so that I would be empowered to focus on more important matters like getting a good education and finding a stable career. Either way her position of seniority wasn't enough to influence or change my mind about his inappropriate conduct towards me. I had seen enough of this level of ignorance to know better.

African Ambiguity: Spring 2001

Lizzy was an attractive girl whose parents migrated from Egypt to the UK in the late 1970s. We were in the same Sociology class I found this subject to be the most interesting of all the course I chose to study that semester. Our teacher Mrs Heath was fun as she steered us through the syllabus in preparation for our exams. She allowed us to reflect on our personal lives in order to make sense of the sociological theories. This was a clever strategy Mrs Heath employed to find out more about our personal backgrounds and beliefs. Nevertheless we were challenged to think quite critically about sociological themes.

The class was one of the few places where race was discussed at school. Mrs Heath presented herself as a liberal woman. She seemed like quite a genuine and open minded person. We used to have debates about perceptions of race. Mrs Heath seemed to have an understanding about how the concept of blackness was viewed in a predominately white environment. She gave an example of the difference between a racist white skin head wearing a t-shirt adorned with the words 'white power' across his chest and a black man wearing a t-shirt saying Black power. Mrs Heath let the class know why these images were incomparable because the advertisements of racial pride didn't hold the same connotations. Mrs Heath's analogy was that the Black man's statement was about building his self-esteem as a member of a subordinate community with minority status in a white westernised environment.

Mrs Heath described how the affirmation of Black Power would be used to promote a positive sense of self and as a reminder that his blackness still mattered and was of value in an atmosphere where members of his community had been marginalised. I thought it was quite admirable for Mrs Heath to acknowledge and reiterate this view. I was thoroughly impressed as most teachers wouldn't have been able to share this with us even if they knew it was the truth. She let us know that for the man who was promoting 'White power' he was doing so as part of a societal system where he was already in an advantageous position. An environment where he could readily attune and align himself to his privilege. Images of his whiteness were promoted positively and were present in some of the highest positions in society. He therefore didn't need to promote it with a

T-shirt. He simultaneously advertises his pride in his whiteness, he simultaneously expresses his hatred for people who are not white. I was taken aback by Mrs Heath's ability to articulate this because it demonstrated her tenacity for viewing race in a way that most white people were unable.

In reference to Lizzy. She is what the media would describe as racially ambiguous, it would be virtually impossible for anyone (with the exception of her fellow Egyptians) to predict what her ethnic origins were. Sure enough her skin was very light, a little bit tanned. But it was evident that she had some colour in her bloodline. The difficulty stemmed from establishing the specific type. I guess Lizzy didn't have to think about her race until she was a teenager and she was required to find out where she fit in society's racial hierarchy.

At the beginning of one of our sociology classes Lizzy sent a sheet around the class room asking each of us to place a tick inside one of the boxed. The sheet looked something like this:

What am I?

White   Black

☐   ☐

I suspected that Lizzy's enthusiasm and curiosity to establish how she would be racially defined was triggered by a long debate we had after a class a few days before. My stance on the matter was that regardless of how light her skin was, as an Egyptian she wasn't exactly white. I knew that skin colour wasn't the only characteristic that was factored in when deciding how a person should be racially identified. A few class mates agreed because the skin complexions of people of different races tend to overlap. There was a Chinese girl in our class who had skin lighter than Lizzy. By no means did this mean that Jia-Lin was white.

When Lizzy's sheet had been sent round the class room and arrived at my desk I inspected it before making my selection. I wasn't at all surprised to see that the majority of our class mates had ticked the white box in comparison to the Black selection.

Predictably I ticked the Black box without hesitation. Once that bit of paper rotated around the room Lizzy was eager to know our thoughts.

'Who ticked Black and who ticked white?'. The responses to her question were inaudible because we all tried to speak at once. Lizzy couldn't see who had been accountable for their choices.

'Who ticked white? Put your hand up'. The majority of hands in the room were raised to confirm they had done so.

'Now who ticked Black?' myself and two other girls raised their hands. The burning question that everyone wanted to know was how and why Lizzy could be identified as Black.

'She originates from Africa. Therefore she cannot be white. How is that possible?' This was a rhetorical question that myself and two other Black girls fired towards our class mates. In our view Lizzy was a person of colour. If there had been a mixed raced box to tick then I would have done so because Lizzy had a racially mixed background. As that wasn't available the Black box in my opinion was the most viable option. Alesha, a fellow West African protested against my judgement. She was adamant that Lizzy was white and that her light complexion solidified this claim.

This was a very heated debate for 16 year old students to be engaged in. Nevertheless it was an important one. Our views about race would continue to be an important factor in our lives, one of which would shape our perspectives of the world. I find it quite amusing. I feel the same way today as I did back them. The points I was reiterating about Lizzy's ethnicity wasn't a view I created and cultivated. This was a widely shared belief. Once upon a time the one drop rule existed and by this definition Lizzy was indeed Black. The criteria of the exclusive one drop sentiment still exists today. If we look at people in the public eye like Mariah Carey, Vin Diesel and Wentworth Miller. They may look white but the fact they have African ancestry means they are regarded as people of colour. At times they have even been labelled Black. They are usually referred to as white when people fail to recognise that one of their parents is Black and/or a person colour.

If Lizzy was granted the opportunity to assimilate into a white realm of existence then that was her choice. Whether it meant denying her Egyptian heritage or not.

As a close friend once told me .

'In this society you must get in where you fit in'.

Educated Fool: December 2002/ January 2003

I had just returned from a four week vacation to Ghana. Marianna and I were having a conversation about my trip and I was explaining how I'd celebrated Christmas with my extended family. My mum had brought live chickens from Kumasi Central market which my aunty later used to garnish our evening meal of fufu and light soup.

Step by step I described the process of how my aunt slaughtered the chicken. My classmate frowned disapprovingly despite the fact that she was a meat eater too.

'So you had a truly Nigerian Christmas' Mr Carlisle smirked as he walked past our table to hand out the class worksheets. I looked up at him. He slipped his petite hands into the pockets of his cheap grey polyester suit. Marianne and I were given the last two hand out sheets which gave him the audacity to stop at our table and interrupt our conversation.

'I'm not Nigerian sir' I replied as I rolled my eyes. I couldn't recall how many times the teaching staff at my school referred to me as a Nigerian. I presumed this meant it was recorded on my school file which may have been the reason why they continued to make the mistake. They simply couldn't be bothered to understand that Ghana and Nigeria had very different cultural practices although they are neighbouring countries.

'I'm not Nigerian, but Marianne is' I pointed to my colleague who sat beside me in silence. Her head lowered down as she had begun to make a start on the written task we were assigned that day. Mr Carlisle started to frown.

'Surely she must be Nigerian and something else. She's not dark enough!' he added.

Marianne's head raised up as she was forced to pay attention. We looked at one another in bemusement. We needed to be sure that we had both heard the same statement being uttered from Mr Carlisle's pencil thin lips. I stared into his eyes as I tried to detect whether there was any evidence of regret or sympathy in his glance. He remained silent and his facial expression was surprisingly calm, it was as if he felt believed that his response was a logical one. I'll be honest. I can't remember how I responded to his statement. But I was concerned that a man who was as educated as my teacher could be so uniformed and narrow minded. Wasn't he aware that Black people have a range of different skin complexions? There are people outside of African who have very dark skinned such as the indigenous tribes in Australia and many Sri Lankan people in southern Asia. These groups aren't necessarily Black so to speak.

It's highly likely that Marianne had some European, Chinese or Arab ancestry in her gene pool but it's wasn't anything remotely close enough for her to trace and pin point to a particular family member. Not all light skinned Black people are mixed and not all West African's share the same cultural practices. My teacher was clearly misinformed or perhaps lazy. Had he taken the time out to research this or ask Black people who knew more about these matters then he would have realised that his conclusions were totally inaccurate and irrational.

Two years prior to this incident Mr Carlisle had told me that he would be pleased if I could secure a D grade in my English GCSE examination because he was taking into consideration that English was my second language. I found this statement particularly offensive. Unfortunately I was not able to speak my mother's tongue which is the dialect Twi (spoken by the Akan tribe in Ghana). Looking back his attitude towards race, more specifically Black people was very peculiar.

What difference would it have made if I spoke Twi at home? The majority of the girls in my school were multi-lingual. Mr Carlisle believed that speaking a second language outside of Europe could be seen as a hindrance and minimise my chances of achieving a decent grade in English Language and Literature. The other girls who spoke other European languages were not patronised in this way. He was convinced that because I spoke another language at home it would limit my capacity to achieve a top grade in English. There are millions of people who are bi-lingual who have the ability to coherently read, write and speak English. My family members in Ghana can do the same, a few can speak French too. Mr Carlisle was the head of the English faculty at the school therefore he should have made a better judgement. Despite being an academically educated man Mr Carlisle was completely clueless. He continued to make assumptions about me based upon my cultural back ground.

Mr Carlisle expectations of my academic capabilities were exceptionally low in this situation. More importantly my aspirations for myself were high. I knew I could no longer seek acceptance and encouragement from people who had very little faith and confidence in my abilities. I couldn't wait for Mr Carlisle and other narrow minded teaching staff to validate my academic performance regardless of whether they were the ones teaching the class or not. I had a responsibility to myself as a young woman. Particularly a student of colour as statistically we were more likely to leave school without any qualifications in comparison to students of other races. Take young Black males for example. Over the years there has been much debate about their attainment as there are a disproportionally large rate of Black male students who are excluded from school and do not obtain any formal qualifications.

Mr Carlisle was standing close by when I found a fellow classmates personal statement for a university application which had been left on the desk in the student's communal recreation area.

'I am a white English literature student' was the opening line of the paragraph on the tatty piece of paper that Mr Carlisle was reading from.

'Well it's obviously not yours Natreema' he chuckled as though the comment was funnier than it actually presented itself. No one else around us was laughing. He thought that it would be amusing to remind me that I wasn't white.

I knew that I had to start believing in myself if I was going to make any positive progress in or outside of school.

I was building my confidence nevertheless I was still quite sensitive. I didn't know how to install a racial filter in my mind to protect myself from such foolishness. What this essentially means is that it would have been impossible to challenge every single person who had something negative or prejudice to say about Black people. I would have drained all my energy if I'd dared to try. It wasn't worth it. At 16 years of age I was quite a self-righteous person who couldn't tolerate unjustified statements. My passionate personality stemmed from my expectations to be treated fairly and with respect. As a young Black girl with a loud voice and a painful past, my zest for life and assertive attitude was translated and regarded as aggression. Being big, Black and outspoken was a bad combination in a predominately white space. Ask anyone who has those characteristics and they will most likely produce the same conclusion. I thought I was standing up for what was right. In reality I was being labelled as a trouble maker. A teacher once said to me sarcastically.

'You're the Shop Steward aren't you' she laughed ' I bet you always say they can't treat us like this' she adopted a high pitched tone to imitate my voice whilst placing her hand on her hip as she rocked her large head from side to side. This educated fool of a teacher believed that this was an impression of how I behaved. I was deemed to be a loud mouthed highly strung pupil with a chip on my shoulder. The teachers could be so judgmental which was a little bit dramatic and quite pathetic as we were just children. Most of the things I did and said were to be funny and accepted by my peers. I had no idea that I was being judged so harshly by adults. The most dangerous thing of all was that my grades were falling which meant I was at risk of leaving school without any formal qualifications. I was heading down a path of self-destruction and some teachers were happy to watch me disappear to that point of no return. My fighting spirit kept me going.

How to be Black?

If I were assigned the responsibility of writing an instruction manual to future generations of Black children. I would begin by stating that nobody can really teach you how to be Black! You develop an understanding of your blackness through your daily experiences. As Black people we tend to behave in response to how we are treated by other races. More specifically Europeans.

Why? In the first instance how you feel about your blackness has and will be shaped by others perception of it in relation to their own race. As Black people a large percentage of our history was pilfered and misplaced during and as a result of the slave trade. Back in Africa and other Black kingdoms/civilizations a great deal of our history was disseminated via our elders orally. Unfortunately once families were separated and Blacks were forbidden from retaining their original names (and prohibited from speaking their mother's tongues) our ancestral stories gradually dispersed into thin air.

Subsequently, the information that was documented about Black people is from a predominately European perspective. 'His-Story' (history) is written by the winners. The ruling classes, the elites. This fact may seem unfair, but that is the reality. Black history has been appropriated by those of European descent. Therefore it is important to understand that the history, the present condition and future of Black people is shaped by and within a wider cultural, economic and socio-political context. One of which continues to be dictated by western society.

Our Black identity isn't exclusively based upon our longstanding trends and traditions. There were other racial groups who had an interest in the native lands that we once inhibited such as Africa and Australia. I would also reinforce the notion that being Black isn't essentially descriptive. Blackness it isn't structured upon or defined by what people tell you about your African and/or Black identify. Consequently a large number of us with a stronger cultural awareness who have become more conscientious of our heritage as we mature have learnt the following:

Learning about how you assimilate into the mainstream dominant and quintessentially European sphere of existence isn't based upon what you are told about or how you've been educated about your Black identity. You may discover that your Black identify and a more coherent understanding of it, confronts all the things you haven't been told about it, which are just as important for you to know. Being Black in a sense is prescriptive and not descriptive. The concept of blackness worldwide is reactive in response to the system of white supremacy.

On a much smaller scale look at Afro hair. A substantial amount of Black women (including myself) apply chemical relaxers to straighten their hair and/or weave hair extensions to lengthen it. Concealing the natural texture of their tresses. The hair and beauty industry is worth multi-millions (pounds, Euros and dollars whatever the currency). As Black consumers continue to amend their natural appearance. Westernised ideals of beauty set the universal standards and we as people of colour gravitate towards it accordingly.

The average woman and man of all races don't look like the models and television stars we see in the lime light. Unfortunately for Black people steering towards a more commercial and mainstream European look is particularly dangerous. As we aspire to emulate the appearance of racial group whose physical characteristics differ so greatly from our natural state of being.

The effects of trying to achieve this unattainable standard of beauty are psychologically and physically damaging. To some extent we have deceived ourselves. In turn there are companies who capitalise on this desperation and our inferiority complex. We must remember that an imitation will never be as authentic as the real thing. No matter how light you are or how light you can become, you can't beat a master at his own game. The only way to look like a European is to be one!

Once upon a time I was an apologetic African. I believed that if my hair was relaxed and I spoke well I would be more accepted by those who called me Black and ugly. I felt there was a chance I could be as pretty as the women on TV. I am glad I came to my senses and repositioned myself into a higher state of consciousness. I fought this battle against myself. I tried so desperately to conform. In my blackness I wanted to achieve a westernised concept of beauty. Aged 12 my mum gave me permission to get my first hair relaxer. For the very first time my best friend who was a white girl wanted to play with my hair. In all the years we had known each other she had never asked to do so before.

I watch television today. I see musicians of different races. The image of blackness strongly exists in the mainstream media, however it continues to be marketed without the use of Black people. Artists like Justin Timberlake, Iggy Azalea, Miley Cyrus, Justin Bieber, Kesha and Rita Ora have sold millions of records globally. They perform pop music with R&B undertones, much of which has been composed and arranged by the hottest African American producers. Often it is a case of Black music being advertised with a white face. These artists are cool. You would be forgiven for making the assumption that their melodic vocals belong to a person of African descent, which makes the act more of a novelty.

In April 2014 Rita Ora visited a New York based Urban Radio station to promote her new music material. The radio host asked Ora (who is British by way of nationality) to clarify her ethnicity. She confirmed that she originates from Albania in Eastern Europe. The hosts addresses the widely shared belief amongst audiences and fans that Ora is Black. The musician is amused by the claim and thanks her gracious hosts for the compliment. She likes the thought of being considered to be a Black person. Ora roared with laughter as she declared that being thought of as Black gets her places.

There perhaps aren't as many authentically Black people who would say or believe that their blackness has afforded them better prospects in life. Nonetheless Ora as a white woman believes so. This was a publicity stunt which demonstrates the clever marketing strategies employed by her record label who have projected the image of racial ambiguity for their artist to flaunt and brag about. I find this insulting and totally aggravating. I don't witness Black people receiving these type of accolades for encompassing a state of being that comes naturally to us. However Ora (much like Timberlake, Bieber, Cyrus, Azalea and Kesha) glorify their affiliation with Black culture which they have actively appropriated in order to make blackness digestible to the white masses. This isn't new. The Rolling Stones, David Bowie (I'm a fan of Bowie!) and most notably Elvis Priestley did this many years ago. They had the force, popularity, financial backing and white acceptability which enabled them to take Black music to places that it had never gone before. The top of the popular charts!

For many years Bowie has vocalised inequality in the music industry. In an interview in he did in the early 1980s when MTV USA launched, he questioned the host about why the channel failed to play the music videos of Black artists. In response the rep was honest about the fact that the majority of audiences were white and would be likely to resists seeing images of Black people on their screens. This is questionable. There were many Black musicians selling millions of records at the time. Perhaps MTV were exercising their power to be ethnically exclusive by sending a clear message to people of colour. For those who lived in Britain in the year 2000 you may recall hearing about a documentary entitled Black like Beckham. The programme (which didn't feature the footballer) presented viewers with accounts made by Z list celebrities (amongst other unknown people) and their debates about the reasons why footballer David Beckham was regarded as an honorary Black man. The list of foolish excuses were endless. These ranged from the cornrows he once wore, to Beckham's taste in R&B music in addition to the unusual names he gave his children and the fact he named his dogs Puff and Snoop. At the time of the programme was broadcast I was in secondary school. I remember my friends and I discussing how stupid it was. A few weeks ago as I was in the midst of writing the Melanin Monologues I surfed the web in search of the footage. I hadn't seen it the first time round. After watching the crap-umentary my feelings hadn't changed. This was a complete mockery of Black culture. Nine times out of ten the behaviour of those who aren't Black but are thought to perform 'like Black people', tend to do so in a stereotypical way. Blackness is interlinked with ones ability to wear cornrows, gold teeth, bling bling, loosely fitting sportswear and emulate street slant or speak in street slang. The positive replications of Blacks by other races very rarely seems to see the light of day when it comes to quote on quote acting Black.

I am sure many would agree when I declare that blackness is more than just an attitude. Blackness is a way of life because it represents communities of people across the globe. The cultural and traditional practices of Black people vary according to the geographical location that one resides. I am sure there are plenty who would also agree that for people of Black ancestry who have Black/darker skin complexions there is no escaping our heritage. We can't opt in and out of our Blackness or put it back in the closet as though it is an item of clothing that is no longer in fashion. Perhaps it's our inability to deactivate our Blackness that makes being Black less exciting for us than it does for famous Europeans like Rita Ora.

From my own perspective I hadn't thoroughly realised what blackness meant until I reached my mid-20s. Metaphorically I compare this learning process to sitting an examination before attending the classes that are needed to successfully prepare for and pass the test. What I am trying to say is that I had to make mistakes about my awareness of race before I had enough knowledge to pass the test. The evidence that I gather from these race related experiences was then applied to the logic I needed to acquire in order to obtain a concise interpretation of what it all meant. I became enlightened about my racial/ethnic identity in reverse. I am not necessarily referring to my heritage as a West African woman. I refer to my position as a Black skinned person in a western society. The countries where our ancestors settled acts as a point of reference for Black people because for many (especially African Americans and those of West Indian descent) it's the furthest that we can trace our lineage back to. On a superficial level when I am discussing Black identify I am mainly referring to the complexion of skin.

My inspiration for writing these monologues has derived from the confusion and embarrassment I've felt about my Black skin since childhood. Sometimes it takes one thing to happen in your life to initiate a wider change. One day I asked myself why am I missing? Why do I belong to a subordinate group? If you have little pride in where you come from then you will never want to claim it. When I was at school very few Black people wanted to associate themselves with Africa. I was undeniably African based upon the unusual type of name I had and a very dark skinned face. Everything about me was so African!

The majority of children of West Indian descent would not embrace the African continent as their ancestral home land and the lighter skinned African children with European surnames would denounce their African lineage. This was occurring in the playground. Unfortunately on a wider scale this is what was happening amongst our parents. This type of division was enforced upon us by our parents and grandparents, much like a form of generational curse and belief system.

Ancient Egyptian culture has been appropriated and disseminated as closely related to Roman and Greek history.

Richard King (Melanin: A Key to Freedom, 1991) analysed the Ancient Egyptians perception of blackness as follows 'Ancient Africans of Kemet so valued their Black skin, there was a prohibition against altering it'. King proceeds to explain how 'melanin [known as] Khem, the khemtic name for Black was seen as having magical properties under the name Jet (Christ)' (p.17).

Rudolph Windsor (In Babylon to Timbuktu, 1988) 'many of the Arabs are not black today because of the crossing of white slaves in their households and harems' (.p37).

How can anyone be ashamed to be from African? In present day the continent is a force to be reckoned with. I am not suggesting that you should disregard what you see advertised on TV. Charities work and organise ways to make money because it is a part of their promotional campaign to draw in further financial support from new and existing customers. The imagery of famine is one small aspect and representation of Africa. Audiences are not educated about the quantity of natural resources that Africa holds in the depths of her soil. The continent has resources in abundance!

Without Africa the mobile phone that you spoke on today, the lap top you typed with or kindle you might have read this book on wouldn't exist. Gold, oil, rubber, titanium. Petroleum, diamonds amongst other precious resources are cultivated and extracted from the African landmass.

Africa has a plentiful fresh water supply with large lakes, big rivers, vast wetlands and limited by widespread groundwater. However only a small percentage of

Africa's available fresh water is currently being used. Four percent according to (Dovi, Africa Renewal Online, 2007).

Now repeat the words Africa, Africa, Africa. If you are Black (particularly of West Indian, African American and South American descent). Africa didn't just produce you and your ancestors, the motherland continues to supplement the world's material needs. The world needs African to sustain its economy, infrastructure, manufacturing good and industries. Before you separate yourself from Africa think very carefully about that!

Home is Africa

As an African I'm proud to be
A tree grown from the strongest seed.
The beauty of a land that gleams
So home is Africa to me.

Carbon coloured like the darkest sky
I couldn't deny it even if I tried
The land that bore my ancestry
Because home is Africa to me.

I was born and raised in London town.
Yet people guess without a doubt
'You're Ghanaian right?' it's plain to see
That's why home is Africa to me.

No matter where I go or how I speak
It's evident from those I meet
The motherland has roots that run so deep
So home is Africa to me.

Heathrow: January 2003

My family and I had arrived at Heathrow airport on a cold wet morning. I remained in the spirit of the Ghanaian New Year's celebration and opted to wear a traditional black and white dress for the journey home. My mum and brothers stuck to a more westernised style of dress code. We were stopped by an immigration officer who asked us to step aside. I was carrying a Ghana must go bag (a red, white a blue bag made of fabric which is typically used in Britain to carry washing to the Laundromat). I dropped the heavy load to the floor. At first I hadn't realised what was happening or why he had stopped us out of all the people who were shuttling through customs.

I recognised this immigration official from a series I used to watch on British television called Airport. He would interrogate people who were entering the UK in order to determine whether they intended to work and settle in Britain illegally.

'Do you normally live in the UK?' he asked my mum who was now frowning. He was stopping us because he'd made the assumption that I (with my African looking face, traditional attire and a Ghana must go bag) was born and bred in Britain.

'Yes. Why have you stopped us out of all these people?' my mum protested. I saw his eyes widened and his jaw drop when he heard her speak in a British accent. That's when I noticed that we were being stereotyped. His face said it all. He was becoming very defensive and I think this is the moment that he'd realised his mistake but he had to keep the act going.

'Can I see your passports?' my mum angrily opened her leather hand bag to retrieve our passports.

'I don't understand why you are stopping us?' she moaned yet did as was instructed to by the immigration officer. Within a matter of seconds she pulled out four British passports. I watched the immigration officer's face transform from white to the same burgundy shade of our passports. His lowered his head towards the floor. He was truly embarrassed to say the least. He took a quick glance at the passport on the top of the pile and handed them back to my mum.

'Okay you can move along'

'I don't know why you stopped us?' my mum said.

'That's fine. I said you can move along!' he demanded. What else could he say? I was slightly offended but I recognised that people saw me as a West African woman before they thought of me as a British citizen. That's fine it doesn't bother me. I find the misconceptions about my behaviour that are made on the basis of these assumptions to be the most annoying. The officer was so focused upon the way I looked that he hadn't even considered that I may have a legal right to remain in the UK. Where I was born and my family had lived for many years! I was frustrated by the fact that in the time he had taken to stop and question my family he had let other people slip through who had no intention of returning home to the country's where they were legal residents. Yet because they didn't look so African they didn't arouse any suspicion.

Lee, South London: 2004

My mum and brothers were parked outside a telephone box in Lee, South-London. We were trying to make a call to Ghana. I was standing at the pay phone as my brother Ray (four years my junior) kept running back and forth between the car and the telephone box to get more coins from my mum so that I could keep speaking to our cousin.

After no more than 10 minutes I completed the call and returned to the car to find that it was surrounded by two men and two women. I immediately knew that they were plain clothed police officers because they were wearing their radios and black body shields. I entered the passenger side of the car as they were walking away from the driver's side of the vehicle and returning to their unmarked saloon car.

'What's going on?' I asked my mum. The windows of her brand new Honda Civic were wound down.

'The police wanted to question me and Ray. They were trying to open the car door' she replied as though she were still in shock.

'What?' I said as I was desperately trying to get a grasp of what she was telling me.

As we were talking the police pulled up alongside us in their car. The windows were still open. The driver was making a comment to my mum. I can't remember the specific words he used but it was loosely apologetic. To some degree he was justifying the reason why he thought my 14 year old brother and mother were raising suspicion in the neighbourhood. I couldn't figure out how a mother and her young children (my nine year old brother Caldeen present) sitting in a car beside a call box looked suspicious? I wondered why nobody thought to ask us whether we were making a call because our car may have broken down. I was extremely upset.

'You stopped my brother because you saw a Black boy walking on the street who you thought looked suspicious' I wailed before I yelled the words 'RACIST!'. I was so annoyed and sincerely felt like we had been judged and patronised. My brother was just a kid who was walking to the pay phone to provide me with coins and standing around as he waited for me to finish the call. He was simply bored. The policeman who was the driver of the unmarked car was infuriated by my accusation.

'Excuse me!' he shouted at me 'you would have been grateful if you were getting mugged' his veins in his temples were visible.

'Is that your daughter?' he asked my mum who sat at the steering wheel in silence.

'We're doing our job' he added. This is the first time in my life I can recall mum being so silent. She would normally support me if she knew I was upset for a good reason or she would have at least told me to shut up if she thought I was wrong. My comment had clearly struck a chord with the officer who would have been trained to remain calm in the most adverse situations. However being called a racist touched a deep nerve. For both he and I.

The fact remains. The police do have a difficult job and we as the citizens must give them the respect they deserve as they protect the public. In this instance it is clear that we were being stereotyped as the potential suspect in question was a little kid who wasn't committing any type of offence. In order to approach us without any solid evidence they were clearly making assumptions about us. Occurrences like this were shaping my views about race. I was becoming more and more aware of the fact that sometimes there was no way to avoid being thought of as behaving suspiciously when you had Black skin.

London Metropolitan University, Aldgate: 2005

Emily was a friendly and pretty blue eyed girl I'd met at Uni. She lived in Hertfordshire in a town a few miles away from Enfield, North London. She spent a year on the course before leaving to pursue a different career. We got on incredibly well. We were exactly the same age. She was the kind of patient, mild-mannered girl that I would have made friends with at secondary school.

Emily was a very sweet person but the fact she hadn't ever lived in a multi-cultural environment reflected in her views about race. There had only been one Black girl in her entire school who had arrived in her sixth form year. The girl had come from Ghana to study in the UK. Emily would tell me about the similarities between this girl and I, with the exception of one thing.

'You're very English aren't you?' Emily said to me as we sat together waiting for our lecture to begin. I didn't have a Ghanaian accent and I was able to share Emily's memories of the music, film and television programmes that she had watched and enjoyed as a kid. We would often reminiscence about these things. Therefore in Emily's mind this meant that I had a strong understanding of things that were quintessentially English.

Emily's long term boyfriend was Asian. They are now married and have a beautiful little girl. A great deal of what she learnt about race and people of colour was gathered through this relationship. From what I could see she didn't have a realistic view of what was going on in a vibrant city like London especially when it came to different racial groups living amongst one another.

Then we got talking about Brixton (a town in South-West London). Emily seemed to hold many misconceptions about the district.

'If me and my boyfriend were walking through there hand in hand would we be stared at?' she asked naively.

Emily seemed to think that Brixton was a dangerous neighbourhood. I could understand why. The media's representation of the area and the negative legacy of the quote on quote 'riots' (1981) was itched into people's memories and perpetuate these types of beliefs.

'Nobody would notice or care for that matter' I clarified. In reality she wouldn't have looked out of place with an Asian man in Brixton. There were so many interracial couples living there at the time. The same can be said more than a decade later. Nevertheless I knew that it would be difficult to convince Emily that Brixton wasn't at all like she had read about, but if she wasn't willing to go and see it for herself then this view wouldn't change. I could only imagine some of the myths she had heard about Brixton from friends and family who hadn't even been to the area themselves.

Emily and I were about 20 years old at the time and she had been with her boyfriend for over five years. She correctly predicted that they would eventually get married. Emily felt confident enough to share her private views about mixed relationships with me. I admired her honesty.

'I know that my little girl will never look like me. She will never have blue eyes or fair skin'. Emily was fully aware of the dynamics of race and how people of colour hold the dominant gene. She knew it was likely that any children she produced with her Asian partner would most likely resemble his side of the family. She loved her boyfriend very much but this was quite a difficult thing to come to terms. But Emily accepted it would be inevitable. I think what she was trying to say (in the politest way possible without offending me or looking as though she was racist) was that her children could never be white. They could only be classified as mixed raced or Asian. Emily was a lovely girl and seems to be happily married. She has been with her partner for more than 12 years. The couple are well equipped to deal with any challenges that being an interracial couple may bring. They have a lot more experience than most. In the end their love should help them overcome it.

Aspirations of Assimilation, Goldsmiths College: Autumn 2006

British universities tend to attract students from all parts of the world. I found it to be an exciting environment because it really opened my mind to different perspectives on Politics and social sciences. I got partnered with a very beautiful Latina called Jennifer in one of my media relations classes. She was born and raised in New York City. As part of our exercise Jennifer reflected upon the time she spent growing up in a predominately African American community. Her peers constantly referred to her as 'white girl' and I noticed that she kept making the same references to her own race in the same way. Of course the Puerto Rican community is very diverse. Some are Black and many are mixed raced. There are Puerto Ricans who look European a bit like Jennifer Lopez/JLO (post 2001). I think JLO looked more ethnic before she became famous.

Jennifer (my colleague) had the JLO type of Latina look because her European ancestry was slightly more visible than the African or Native Indian. Jennifer told me that her boyfriend was a white British guy. I couldn't help but interject my opinion into Jennifer's views about race. I waited carefully for her to finish her statement. She claimed that her white skin had made her feel ostracized in her community. I think she was so candid with me because she assumed that her beliefs and my definition of her race would mirror the views of her peers in New York.

'Mmmm. That's strange' I said 'you see if I saw you without knowing what your background was I wouldn't have thought that you were white. To me you look like a person of colour' I added and waited patiently for Jennifer's reaction. She smiled and giggled nervously.

'Okay' she replied calmly. The olive skin of her large forehead in between her perfectly plucked eyebrows creased.

'In my neighbourhood they called me white' she stated in an attempt to demonstrate how and where the view of her ethnicity emerged. Jennifer may have been white in a Black community setting but I had a basic understanding of the history of Latin Americans. JLO's popularity in the mainstream charts inspired much debate about the legacy of Latin American culture and how their ancestry was a combination of Black African, European and Native Indian heritage. With this knowledge Jennifer and I both knew that she wasn't the 'white girl' she claimed to be. I explained to Jennifer the things I had noticed about racial categorisation in Britain.

'In this country people may call you white because they have a tendency to define peoples race by the colour of their skin and features' she folded her arms and I suspected she couldn't fully grasp what I was trying to say, so I went onto emphasise my point in order to try and make her understand.

'Your skin is very light' I stated the obvious and she nodded in agreement 'almost, if not the same colour as many Europeans. But you're racially mixed'. I thought it was necessary to interject a visual example.

'Have you seen the 80s film Flashdance with Jennifer Beals? Her dad is African American yet to this day people think that she is white Italian or Irish'. Jennifer shrugged and perched her lips together. She may not have liked or agreed with what I was saying but she most definitely understood my point.

People of colour tend to have a radar where they can see colour in those who try and pass for white. My colleague's dark brown eyes, button nose and freckles as well as her thick black hair made it clear to me that she was of mixed origin. Maybe she felt I wouldn't see these features because I was comparing her skin tone to my dark complexion.

When the lecturer demanded our attention and we had to feed our discussions back to the class Jennifer raised her hand to volunteer to speak.

'Well I'm white. Growing up in my neighbourhood…..' she babbled on like she was reading from a scripted teleprompter. I glanced around the room to see whether I could capture anyone else's reaction and see if they agreed or disagreed with her account. The faces were blank which suggested that their feelings were indifferent.

I thought Jennifer's aspirations to assimilate into the realm of whiteness were quite interesting. Admittedly she could have readily passed for an Italian, Spanish or Greek woman. Was Jennifer trying to convince herself that she was white and promote her new identity in Britain? I believe that she was. Somehow her confidence in the ability to be white was questionable. I had yet to meet a single European who had to declare their whiteness in the way Jennifer had that day. For that would be stating the obvious. Authentically white people need not state what the world can already see. If Jennifer went onto marry her British boyfriend and remained in England I've no doubt that she would tick the white box in the section of an application form used to classify ones racial identity. Good luck to her. If the shoe fits then why shouldn't she wear it? A white world may present her with opportunities that would have been denied to her as a Latina in America.

Goldsmiths College, London: Spring 2006

Farrah had spent a few years touring Europe before she settled in London to complete her MA. I was one of the few students enrolled on the course who was born and raised in London. I enjoyed being on campus because it gave me a chance to meet people from every single corner of the world. I learned that Farrah originated from Egypt. I wouldn't have known otherwise. I thought she was Greek. There were a number of students I'd met from Greece at the time.

We were waiting in the hallway for our lecture to begin as we immersed ourselves in a conversation about Africa. I spoke of my desire to visit Egypt one day.

'We have that African connection' I joked and we both giggled. A young lady with a blunt bob hair style interrupted our conversation.

'Where are you from?' she asked Farrah as though she had to find out as a matter of urgency. I thought she was quite rude. She was the type who would never smile or talk to me despite us being in some of the same classes together. This was quite unusual as the majority of students were friendly. There were quite a few group tasks set as part of the assessment so people were more inclined to build alliances. I wondered how she had the audacity to interrupt my discussion. You see her curiosity had gotten the best of her she had lost herself for a moment. Farrah appeared white and this student needed to know what connection Farrah had with a dark skinned Black African like myself.

The bobbed haired bandit interrogated Farrah and completely ignored me. I turned my back on her and let her carry on talking. She seemed very ignorant to me. For if she truly understood the racial and cultural diversity of the African continent then Farrah's ethnicity wouldn't have come as much of a surprise to her.

African Arrival

I would be a multi-millionaire if I had received £1 for every time someone commented on how well I speak English for an African person. Or if I were paid each time some asked me how many years I've lived in Britain. Subsequently I've had to view myself through the eyes of others when these types of statements and questions have been thrown my way based on people thinking that I have just arrived from Africa.

The other day a friendly Egyptian man made an attempt to chat me up as I crossed the road on my way to work.

'You look like Naomi Campbell' he chimed. This was a very sweet gesture but my waist is twice the size of Naomi's and I am virtually a foot shorter than her. Tariq wanted to take me out for a drink but I was running late so I politely declined his offer. He told me that he was working as an electrician in a local company. He asked what I did for a living.

'What are you doing in London?' he wanted to know.

'I was born here' I replied without hesitation. After we went our separate ways I thought about the question Tariq had fired at me. What was I doing in London? Nobody had ever asked me that before. What am I doing in London? I asked myself because I'd never thought about it before.

Tariq's question reminded me of the day I'd accompanied my sister to a hair salon where her friend worked. I was about 19 then. One of the middle aged friends of the owner (known as Oga) Sam was desperate to know more about me.

'Did she just come from Ghana?' he nodded his head towards my seat. He didn't seem to want to ask me the question directly. I'm not sure why. Oga Sam hadn't contemplated that I'd completed secondary school before his Visa application had been accepted and cleared for entry in the UK from Nigeria. He had not long arrived in Britain from Africa himself. I know he wasn't trying to be malicious but he was being ignorant. Both instances remind me that although I was born and brought up in the UK there were times when I felt as if I didn't belong here. People seemed to constantly question my citizenship, it was really annoying.

Whilst studying for my undergraduate degree a on campus at London Metropolitan University I was asked by Maija, a mixed raced lady of Danish and Gambian heritage.

'Where are you from? She enquired in her softly spoken voice.

'Lewisham' I instinctively uttered as everyone else was referring to the town they had chosen to inhibit for the duration of their studies in the UK.

'Noooo' she shook her head in disapproval.

'Where are you from?' she replied. I knew she was trying to extract the conscious version of this answer. Nobody is ever interested in the fact that I was born in South London. However it's the explanation they require when needing to justify why I speak English so fluently and without any regional accent, so to speak.

I once stood in a bank in Lewisham one afternoon waiting in the queue. Without opening my mouth two boys with neatly trimmed fade haircuts and matching brown complexions, laughed amongst themselves as they stood behind me waiting for the ATM.

'That's fresh of the boat' the shorter of the two guys concluded about my nationality. This was a derogatory term used to describe people who have recently arrived in the UK from sub-Saharan Africa (Black Africa). The categorisation suggests that the person is quite uncivilized and has yet to adjust or adopt westernised standards of living. They failed to see that I could spot them from the corner of my eye, I knew I was the source of their jokes. Or maybe they didn't care. Would it have mattered if I'd just arrived in the UK as they had assumed? Those ignorant fools wouldn't ever know that I could speak English better than the two of them put together. My dark skinned face and the head wrap I wore appeased their assumption about my immigration status.

FOTB is an acronym used by young people for the term Fresh of the boat. My brother made a point I couldn't disagree with when I told him about what happened in the bank that day.

'I don't understand why they think they've got the right to call us FOTBS' he was referring to the long standing banter between West Indians and Africans.

'They're the ones who came off a bloody boat' I wasn't sure whether he was referring to the slave boat that transported from Africa to the Caribbean Islands and the

Americas or ships like the Windrush which docked from the West Indies to the UK in the late 1940s. In any case he did have a point.

The Name Game : Winter 2007

Finding work after I completed my Masters degree was proving to be a challenge. I didn't know what I wanted to do or where I would comfortably fit in. I managed to get a job at a market research company in Elephant and Castle which paid about £6.50 per hour. I was happy to be working and saving part of a small salary.

The team I was based in were working on a project that meant we had to call bank customers and obtain their feedback on the service. I interviewed some really polite people. There were times when I'd be sworn at and verbally abused. One guy made a sexual proposition to me. In any case I knew it wasn't personal, customers were fed up of being inundated with telephone calls. Many of them were small businesses and just wanted to be left alone. Their lives were busy enough.

A single working shift was three hours long. In that time employees were required to have four completed interviews. If our targets were not met we wouldn't get booked for any more shifts the following week. The company operated on a 0 hours contract so they had the flexibility to let employees go at any given time. The work was stressful you had to be focused, charming and a quick writer to survive. We had to record customer's feedback verbatim in handwriting. Then type it up later, it was quite tedious. During my four month stint at the company I learnt some very thought provoking things about race. The majority of my colleagues were Black and Southern Asian. Management were white and team leaders (a few were Black), the majority were white and the rest belonged to other racial groups (mixed race, Mediterranean). That's how the employee structure was composed.

We had to provide our first and last names to customers when we were conducting interviews. I was very unhappy about that because I felt it compromised my personal safety. I noticed four weeks into my new job that I was getting better responses and more completed interviews when I introduced myself to customers with an English sounding surname. My real name sounded like two surnames according to some of the people I spoke to. In my sixth week I took on the persona of Charlotte Smith. At the beginning of each interview I introduced myself as Charlotte and without fail I met my targets on every shift. Sometimes I secured a record breaking six completed interviews.

Regardless of whether the customers responded more openly to me because they believed they were speaking to a British or even white woman is debatable. Not all the customers were white. But the fact still remains, as Charlotte Smith I became the highest achieving telephone interviewer. Our team leaders monitored our interviews from the back office. One afternoon I was approached by a manager who praised my performance but criticised some of the methods I implemented as I engaged with the customer.

'That was very good. By the way what's your name?' he began to tick a few boxes on the sheet of paper that was attached to his large clipboard. I replied and he frowned.

'Why are you calling yourself Charlotte Smith?'.

'I wasn't getting as many responses when I was using my real name'.

'Okay well you can't do that. You'll have to use your real name from now on'.

I agreed and he told me that my performance would be monitored before he walked off. I had to work twice as hard with an ethnic sounding name. I wasn't ashamed of my name , I'd always loved the fact that I could boast that my mother had created it for me before I was born. But I wanted to do whatever it took to make money. I thought more about cash than I did my integrity and maybe I was lacking confidence.

A few days later I overheard a conversation taking place between Ayo who was one of the team leaders and Rose, a senior manager. Ayo resembled Ray J (brother of the singer Brandy, he was infamous for making the sex tape with Kim Kardashian). Ayo was a handsome young Nigerian guy and Rose a feisty middle aged white woman who managed the entire operation.

'I've put Abdul on a different project' Ayo moaned.

'Why?' Rose asked abruptly

'The bank project. Nobody would speak to him. It's because he's Nigerian. They don't trust him. The whole 419 thing' Ayo explained. Rose cleverly remained silent. There was not much else she could say. Agreeing with Ayo would have made her appear racist but the fact she didn't challenge Ayo's decision was an indication that she solemnly agreed with it.

'I'm Nigerian' Ayo declared breaking their awkward silence 'and I wouldn't trust him either'. Ayo's admission made me smile because I knew I wasn't imaging things or being paranoid. When we made calls people were judging us based on the way we sounded. Our conduct and manner was only part of the focus. The majority of it boiled down to where they thought we were from. In my personal life I can always detect when I'm speaking to a person who is Black or Asian whether they were brought up in the UK or have an English accent. There is something about the tone of the voice that makes it obvious to me, it's a deeper voice. I left the company a few weeks later as there was a discrepancy with my pay. The company failed to pay me the extra 50 pence per hour I was entitled to having passed my probationary period.

My Blackness

A hue as deep as its roots.
Reminiscent of the darkest chocolate and the ripest aubergine.
I can't imagine why?
Once a upon a time
It defined my value and self-worth
My name at birth?
Was replaced with ridicules:
Blackie, Blick, Burnt toast, Midnight, Black attack.

There were more insults hurled at me.
Too many to remember.
Words used interchangeably,
With ugly!
I heard them so often.
I believed no one loved me.
I didn't see my Blackness on TV positively
Or on magazines with faces considered pretty.

Really it doesn't matter
I now realise that the sun loves me
That's why he blessed me
With all his energy.
The Blackness of the night sky
Overseeing the entire world
Stares back at me like a reflection
Occupying the space of our very existence.
At the highest height
Like African Royalty.
Even the stars need darkness to shine!

The Blackness I used to despise,
Makes me wise.
Imagine.
The cause of self-hate,
Makes me great.
Life challenged me.
A choice between the bleaching creams,
Or a search for my self-esteem.
I choose my Blackness.
Why wouldn't I?
It's the core part of me.

Black Beauty

The deep routed rejection of darker skin tones in society and the so called inferiority complex (that some of us with darker skin may possess) leads to the assumption that dark skinned people desire to bleach their skin. I have received many compliments about my skin tone. Quite ironically these have been followed by statements demanding that I shouldn't alter my complexion. Somehow I've found a way to be comfortable in this skin, regardless of what the world thinks about it. In this life time I will always possess this hue. No matter what complexion altering creams I buy, there is nothing that can reverse the fact that I am genetically African. That's cool, I've learnt to live with it.

My definition of a racial renaissance is about self-acceptance and realising that I am not just pretty for a dark skinned girl. I am not just very well spoken for a Black girl who was brought up on the grittier side of South London. I am beautiful because I am Black and African. I don't have to possess any other ancestry in my DNA to validate the beauty of my blackness. I can be an attractive person without adhering to the European standards of beauty promoted in the media and perpetuated by the masses, as we aspire to look our best. I speak well because I am intelligent, educated and think reflectively.

I would like people to recognise that an appreciation and love for my own race doesn't equate to me hating another. I can see the goodness in others and recognise their achievements. However I must first concentrate and focus upon matters that affect me directly. I, like many other Black men and women across time have been engrossed in the activities of other ethnic groups so much so that we have ignored the accomplishments and greatness of our own.

Even something as simple as hair. Blonde flowing hair is beautiful. Yes! But I love my natural hair even more. I love its versatility. I can wear it natural without extensions in a kinky afro. I can rock braids and at times I enjoy wearing a weave on. That doesn't make me ashamed of my natural hair and it certainly doesn't mean that I am trying to look white. Even if I were, a white standard of beauty is something that I can never attain. Irrespective of how straight the hair is or how much I've paid for it or which tribe in the Asian or South American continents the hair came from. That type of hair will never grow from my scalp.

As Black people we should remember that we are being inauthentic and we look ridiculous trying to emulate something that isn't a part of our genetic makeup. We need to feel better about being Black. We must empower ourselves and feel comfortable with who we are.

Historically we are creative, innovative, strong and once upon a time Black communities (worldwide) were self-sufficient. Don't believe me? Check your history! This knowledge should give you the confidence to aspire for more than what you have in front of you. Our ancestors did it, even our grandparents did. My grandparents left Ghana to come to Britain. When they arrived the culture was different from anything else they had ever seen. Migrants like my grandparents weren't used to racism. But they survived, found jobs, brought a house and raised my mother! We can improve and develop ourselves. Why not? It's possible. Just try.

Apple Orchard: Summer 2010

New York City was as grand as I'd imagined it to be. Much like my visit to Boston the year before it all seemed surreal. I felt like I was on the set of a movie and that a camera crew would emerge from somewhere around the corner. I'd seen so much of America on television the city felt so familiar to me.

This first trip to the Big Apple with my friend Chantelle (who I met at school) really brought me out of my shell. I was a shy and nervous young woman before. Like me Chantelle was born to Ghanaian parents. We stayed in a hotel on 5th Avenue and West 31st.

We were truly humbled and overwhelmed by the attention we were receiving in the city. On a trip to Ground Zero a handsome middle aged African American army man told us that we were beautiful girls as he gave us directions. The young ticket sellers outside the Empire State Building were mesmerised by our rich complexions. We weren't used to being complimented back home.

I spent an afternoon alone uptown in the Bronx. After visiting the local zoo I took a walk around the local neighbourhood before heading to the subway to return to Manhattan. I waited patiently on the sidewalk waiting for the lights to change so that I could cross the street. I noticed three brothas on the opposite side of the road. I wasn't concerned about being on my own in a neighbourhood I was unfamiliar with. I was more worried that they were going to call me a derogatory name and taunt me about my skin colour. I was petrified. Having been in the city for three days, my confidence was growing. The handsome men I'd come across on my travels were showing me that they found me attractive. I enjoyed every minute of the admiration. The traffic lights changed. I held my breath and started to walk slowly across the street. The guys were getting closer yet I kept my head up and fixed my gaze on a sign post in the distance. We were now in the middle of the street. They were engrossed in a conversation. Then they suddenly went silent for a moment.

'Pretty girl' one of the men sang at me. I was too shy to make eye contact. Another one began to make petting sounds as though he were initiating a kiss. I smiled because I didn't want to seem obnoxious. I wanted to seem polite and not stuck up. When they were out of sight I breathed a sigh of relief and my heart reverted to its regular pace. This reminded me that there were men out there who found dark skinned women like me attractive. Good looking men who had sexual appeal and swagger. The compliments took a while to get used to. I didn't believe I was worthy of them to begin with. I didn't think I deserved to be called pretty or beautiful. The name calling from childhood had deeply damaged myself esteem. I had to look beyond my home town to learn about my beauty. I could shine and thrive somewhere else.

Chantelle and I were adjusting to big city life yet we found the subway system a little confusing. The metro lines are lettered and numbered it was a lot more intricate than the London Underground system where the lines are referred to by their names and colours. Chantelle and I were desperate to see the Brooklyn Bridge. We spent at least an hour riding the subway back and forth yet we kept missing the stop to alight and walk to the site. Somehow we ended up in an underground station in the Sunset Park district. There was litter scattered across the tracks. Rats and mice nibbled away at the debris. The peeling paint from the metal pillars on the platform and station signs indicated that we were miles away from mid-town and its well maintained platforms in Manhattan. We were nervous and lost. Everyone else waiting on the platform was Black. We were clearly in an African American neighbourhood.

'You know why this place looks like this don't you?' Chantelle stared at me with watery eyes 'look around you. Would you ever see a station like this in a white neighbourhood?' This was a rhetorical question I didn't need to add my opinion for Chantelle and I both knew the answer. I wanted to get back to the hotel.

'Y'all from England?' a lady with no front teeth asked us because she had overheard us talking. She had a friendly smile. Her clothing was torn and discoloured. Her appearance made me think of those characters suffering from drug addiction in one of those movies set in the ghetto.

'Yes' we smiled.

'I love your accents. Y'all visiting New York uh?' I nodded.

'Welcome, enjoy yourselves' she said just as the train arrived. She was a very sweet lady but we were in no mood to engage in a conversation. I was so relieved when the train arrived. We seemed to be the only people on the platform from out of town. Everyone was staring at us.

Girl about the Town: June 2011

A year later I returned to New York with my family. I opted to stay in mid-town Manhattan again. On a trip to the MAC cosmetics counter in Macy's department store the Sales Assistant sold me NW58, the darkest shade of the studio fluid foundation. There were only two bottles left, which surprised me. I didn't think it would be such a popular selling product. Apart from the Senegalese women I had come across in Harlem I hadn't seem many people as dark as I on the streets of Manhattan.

'It's because a lot of the Africans come in here and buy this product' the pretty sales rep with rosy cheeks and a caramel complexion smiled at me exposing a set of gleaming white, perfectly aligned teeth. A small orange tinted afro framed her oval shaped face.

She clasped a fresh piece of sponge between her thumb and index finger, dabbing the wedge onto the splotch of liquid foundation on the back of her palm. The fluid changed the beige sponge to a shade of dark brown. She smeared the liquid across the bridge of my nose, fore head and chin before blending it in.

'Your skin is so beautiful' she sighed.

She filled in my eyebrows with a burgundy brow liner and decorated my lips with a pink lip gloss.

When my make over was complete I agreed to purchase the foundation. I didn't walk away with any other makeup samples she had applied to my face as the sharp colours were too bright for me. She returned with a sealed bottle of the foundation.

'My colleague over there' the beautician pointed to a petite light skinned lady, with jet black hair layered into a bob cut and the employee waved in our direction.

'She said you are very beautiful'

'You're beautiful' the petite attendant mimed at me reassuringly with a wide smile.

This time something felt different. I almost believed them. I'd received so many compliments from people I didn't know as I walked the streets. Why would they need to lie to me? They didn't owe me anything. Maybe they were saying these nice things to me because they were true.

Harlem Hospitality: July 2011

My family and I were looking for a soul food restaurant to sample some African America dishes. Navigating through the streets of Harlem was like entering a maze. There were so many blocks. We may have been lost, but I was closely observing my surroundings. More specifically how the people looked, walked and talked. In addition to the cars they were driving and how they dressed. I stared up towards the sky and examined the structure of the multi storey buildings. The wealth of the midtown district certainly wasn't reflected in this part of the neighbourhood. I was getting a serious reality check. There was a reoccurring pattern in pockets of the city. People of colour seemed to live in close proximity to dire poverty.

The most shocking thing I noticed was a queue of people who were standing in the sweltering heat. I assumed that they were waiting to buy a new product or to see a film. As I paced along the side walk I got closer to the front of their line.

'You can have one then you'll have to come back later okay' a light skinned sista handed an elderly woman a box which had some form of leaves peering out of the lid. I gathered my thoughts for a few moments so that I could interpret what was happening before my eyes. The next person in the line was given a box and sent away. I turned back to look at my mum who was a few yards behind me. She was looking directly in my eyes with a pensive stare. There was sadness in her eyes that mirrored the sadness in my heart. I couldn't bring myself to talk about what we had seen until we returned to the hotel hours later. We were on our way to buy food as we saw these people queuing. Perhaps we both felt that it would have been disrespectful to discuss the matter at the time.

The Black people were lining up and waiting for vegetables. The elderly lady I had seen wanted an extra box, but the rationing system meant she had to return later to ensure that everyone could have a fair share. I wrapped my mind around this experience.

Harlem is a few miles away from the diamond district of Manhattan. The people breathe the same air and are governed by the same political administration. The difference in terms of the needs of the people are extreme. They might as well live in two different parts of the worlds. The rich/poor divide seemed to be so wide and followed the same path as divisional colour guidelines between the white, Black and brown communities.

I got my first taste of Harlem when I visited the area in the summer of 2010. Chantelle and I got talking to an African American woman who updated us about the politics of the local community.

'Bill Clinton's administration moved to 125th Street. They making it really fancy round here' she said. There were many more stories I heard about the gentrification of the neighbourhood from true Harlemites who had lived in the district for generations. Harlem is the only home they've ever known. They weren't happy about the prospect of being relocated to another part of the city because the cost of living in Harlem was somewhat extortionate. They were slowly being out priced of the district.

I saw a bit more of Harlem beyond 125th Street on a later visit to New York with my brother in summer 2013. We took the subway from Manhattan, uptown to 148th Street subway station and walked all the way to 125th Street district. There were so many empty plots of land that were ready to be sold for development. In upper Harlem I saw many white people living in the neighbourhood. I'd hardly seen any Europeans in 125th Street prior to this. The wealthy influences in upper Harlem were slowly tricking down into central zone. My brother and I predicted that the next time we'd come to visit this part of Harlem it would be a predominately white neighbourhood.

I remember another trip I took to New York with my family in Summer 2012. We had purchased an open bus ride tour ticket which gave us unlimited journeys across the city for two days. A charismatic elderly white women who reminded me of Betty White from the 1980s sitcom The Golden Girls was our host for the ride. She commentated about the city's most prominent attractions. We were shown the site where Billy Cosby's son Ennis served an internship at Columbia University teachers college in west side Manhattan. Ennis was murdered in the 1990s and our host explained that he had a promising future and ambitions to open a school for children with special educational needs.

When the bus finally reached Harlem and our host asked if anyone wanted to alight the other tourists remained silent.

'Yes' my mother yelled and waved to get the hosts attention. We were the only Black people who just so happened to be willing to get off in Harlem.

'Goodbye, enjoy yourself' the woman's voiced screeched through the bus speakers. In Harlem I felt right at home, amongst a community of people who looked just like me.

Black and Almost Proud, London: August 2011

I met Paul on the fourth floor landing of the office where I'd been working as a personal assistant. He was a young slender brotha of no more than 5ft 8incs, with a flawless caramel complexion. Paul had slanted hazel brown eyes which made him look very pretty but his cool demeanour and deep voice retained his masculine edge. His hair was neatly trimmed into a low cut fade, with a slight wave to its curl pattern which suggested that his ancestral lineage consisted of more than just African blood as it wasn't particularly course in texture.

Paul was undeniably handsome with boyish good looks. I didn't think that he would be attracted to me. I was more accustomed to guys my age teasing me as opposed to fancying me. They tended to go for girls with lighter skin complexions, loosely curled tresses and slender bodies. My appearance defied all these requirements.

One afternoon I trailed hurriedly across the fourth floor towards the lift. I desperately needed to find a functioning printer in the building, in hope of meeting a tight deadline set as part of my secretarial duties.

A few seconds after pressing the call button mounted upon the stone wall, the metallic doors slid open and Paul ascended from the carriage. We locked eyes for more than a few seconds. That's longer than you would normally stare at a strangler unless you were expecting them to say something. He stared intensely at me and I gazed back.

What's his problem? I mumbled to myself, rolling my eyes as I watched him walk away. I wondered whether he would look back to steal a second glance at me. Even then it hadn't dawned on me that this fine looking stranger wanted to make it obvious that he was interested in getting to know me better.

A few days later after I had forgotten about the mysterious colleague. I sat alone in the break out area as I did most lunchtimes. He emerged from the partition that divided the printing hubs from the main office area. He sauntered towards me.

'What's your name?' he asked me confidently without smiling.

I pressed my fingers against my lips and continued to chew.

'Natreema' I mumbled whilst swallowing a large lump of my Beef and Horseradish sandwich.

'I can see you're having lunch' he pointed to the desk of cheesecake, crisps, fruit pieces and carbonated lemon water.

'I will speak to you another time' he added and I smiled. He walked back inside the staff printing area.

A few days later Paul joined me in the printing hub as I completed a task assigned by my manager. He finally introduced himself by name.

'Hi' he nodded and smiled.

'Hello' I said.

Paul asked for my number and I gave it to him. I'm not quite sure why, it just seemed like a reasonable thing to do. We were colleagues after all. I didn't have any intention of engaging in a sexual relationship with Paul.

That very same evening as promised he called. We talked about the laws of attraction and the self-development books we had both read. Our chemistry was strong but not necessarily sexual. As though we had known each other for years. Paul and I laughed and joked but it was getting quite late so he had to go. Admittedly I didn't want him to. There was something intriguing about him. My boyfriend and I had never engrossed ourselves in conversations like this. I was really enjoying Paul's verbal company. But his closing statement of our discussion was quite strange to me.

'There is something of you I'm jealous of '

'What's that?' I wondered but quite strangely had anticipated that he would refer to something about my appearance.

'Your skin colour' he replied without hesitation. He didn't elaborate on the reasons why. Meeting Paul changed the way I thought about myself. This friendship gave me a different understanding of my life. Paul may not be aware of this today, but our first conversation was like an epiphany for me. He planted the seed of self-discovery within my psyche. I was in the midst of a relationship with a male colleague from another department. I chose not to tell my then boyfriend about the newly formed friendship.

Paul made further recommendations. He suggested that I look into the analysis of melanin and research the internet to find out more about its components and how it affects our bodily functions as well as the substances importance to all living organisms.

Paul encouraged me to think of myself as more than just a Black woman, but a spiritual being whose complexion (one of which had made me feel ostracized from other members of my community) was a strength to say the least.

There was so much more information that I hadn't been taught about being a dark skinned woman. Beyond the reoccurring arguments that European standards of beauty are more acceptable in western society.

The skin tone debate, more specifically light skin vs dark skin is so much deeper and more complicated than the superficial opinions relating to its cosmetic value. I had to learn about melanin from a different perspective. The fact that it's an integral part of our very existence. The presence of melanin in our organs determines the strength and operational capacities of our bodily functions as well as how we view ourselves.

As the months went by Paul and I were getting closer as friends. There were times when we would talk all night on the telephone. When my boyfriend ended our brief relationship, Paul was like my rebound relationship without the element of sexual intimacy. He was one of the most attractive men in our office so it came as no surprise that some of the other women of all races fancied him too. Naturally this created some jealousy.

Janine was a chubby mixed raced girl who worked as a project coordinator within the team that Paul was employed in as an assistant. Quite frankly she fancied the pants of him but chose to be cold towards him. We both knew that this was a strategy Janine used to conceal the fact was strongly attracted to Paul. Either way it was unnecessary and uncalled for. Paul would always talk about me to aggravate her. He told me about a time when Janine had given him a lift to work. Paul had expressed his desire to settle down with an educated and kind hearted woman like me. It came as no surprise that she resented the bond that Paul and I shared. According to Paul she had told him that he was 'too nice' to be with a girl like me. Janine couldn't understand why a good looking man like Paul yearned to be with a 'Black' woman like me. Paul and I both agreed that Janine's real issue was that she couldn't fathom how Paul could fancy me and not her. Janine wasn't used to losing a handsome man's attention to a dark skinned Black girl. She didn't regard me as any competition whatsoever. She simply couldn't handle being side lined and it infuriated her.

I didn't take any of her negative comments too personal. I could see that she felt threatened. I was very cautious of her after we had a brief encounter in the female toilets. I was in the mirror combing my Remy weave extensions when Janine walked in.

'You can stop looking at yourself, you're pretty enough' Janine smirked as she entered a cubicle. I hesitantly smiled back. What else could I say knowing that she had been calling me ugly behind my back?

Nancy was another colleague. A pretty brown haired girl with sparkly blue eyes. She was quite friendly with Janine, although I embraced her as a work pal I was incredibly weary of her. In my mind it posed a conflict of interest. I suspected that she had a crush on Paul too. Each time Nancy asked me whether anything was going on between Paul and I my response was always the same.

'We're just friends'. I don't know what else she was expecting me to say? There were times when she mentioned Janine in passing to me. Apparently Nancy had mentioned to her that Paul was besotted by me.

'Yeah sorry we both agreed that you are out of his league' Nancy told me, yet somehow I wasn't convinced by her claim. There was no way on earth I believed that Janine was telling Nancy that I was too good for Paul. Clearly someone had to be lying. Paul warned me that his interest in me shattered Nancy's ego too as we both knew that Nancy was attracted to him as well.

'She doesn't think of Black girl's as any kind of competition' Paul laughed and I imagined that to be the truth about Nancy's feelings. I must have irritated her through the duration of our superficial friendship. Nancy and Janine had boyfriends. Paul and I were both single at the time. I couldn't see what their issue was? If we had gotten together it wouldn't have infringed upon anyone else.

'Damn. They can't stand to see a Black man and woman being happy together' I imitated a Brooklyn style accent to make Paul laugh. But I wasn't kidding. That's what I had observed from the situation. That's how I sincerely felt.

On the train home from work one evening I had told Nancy that the handsome Lebanese man who had worked in neighbouring department had asked me out on a date. Her eyes lit up like fireworks.

'Oohh why didn't you go for it?' she pondered. I was adamant that I would never date someone I worked with ever again, having done so the year before. Within a week I noticed that she had become his friend on Facebook. I could only imagine how she initiated a conversation with him. Once she became aware of the attraction Kyle had for me her jealousy would ensure that any chances of Kyle and I having a friendship or budding romance would be doomed. Jealously is truly an ugly thing.

Instances like this made me feel that there were people who seemed to have a problem with a dark skinned girl getting attention and shining in a world where the spot light rarely focused on her.

Gracious Graham

Graham worked with teenagers who had behavioural problems. His was born in London in the late 1960s to Jamaican parents. We were based in the same department and became friendly. Graham was proud to call himself an African man, he had visited the mother land on several occasions. He took every opportunity to convince me that I was beautiful because he was sure that I felt otherwise. I was a little bit frustrated by this. There was a tendency for people to believe I was suffering from self-hatred based on my complexion. I would say I became a little more suspicious of people after this. Did this mean that they didn't think of me as being as proud as they told me I was?

By the time Graham and I met I knew how to appreciate the beauty of blackness. He inspired me for the fact that he understood the value of Black empowerment.

'Black people are strong' he proudly stated 'look at everything we've been through and we're still here'.

I keep this belief close to my heart. It motivates me to remain focused and chase my dreams. I concluded that if there were Black people across the world who managed to excel, cultivate careers and educate themselves in environments where they have been marginalised then this generation of young people have absolutely no excuses. My ancestors built the foundation and I stand upon their shoulders.

There are times when I have often worried that my dark complexion was a hindrance and would impinge upon my professional development. I was challenged to re-evaluate the limitations that I had set upon myself during after a conversation I had with a friend.

'I don't care about any glass ceilings, I'm Jamaican. I'm breaking through them' Jermaine stated during a conversation we had about Black empowerment.

Different Place, Same Ole Race: July 2012

If you can make it here you can make it anywhere. I suppose. African Americans seemed so much more confident to me. They dared to reach the highest heights. Every Black person I know in the UK has a relative who migrated to the United States and went onto achieve a level of success that has yet to be emulated by any Black Briton I know. With this in mind I was surprised to have received first hand discrimination in the Big Apple. My mother and I along with my two younger brothers shuttled from Manhattan to Brooklyn one sunny Saturday afternoon in hope of fulfilling my brother's dream of crossing the Brooklyn Bridge. It was one of the hottest period in

NYC. We stared at the arches of the bridge standing tall in the distance yet we couldn't seem to get close enough.

After more than an hour trailing bank and forth along Tillary Street it was time to abandon the mission and head back to our hotel in Manhattan. We congregated along the side walk hoping to flag down a taxi cab. Each time we tried a yellow vehicle sped past us. I convinced myself that there must be an unwritten code amongst Brooklynites which prohibited people from hailing a cab in this particular district. The cars continued to accelerate passed us. A further 30 minutes went by before it dawned on me. I squinted my eyes to take a closer inspection of the cars so I could determine why they wouldn't stop. Many of the taxis' were travelling without passengers. Coincidentally those with illuminated lights perched upon the roofs of the vehicles suggested that the drivers were clearly on duty and their vehicles were unoccupied.

We turned into a nearby avenue and sat on the wall to rest our aching feet. We needed to gather enough energy to walk to the next subway station as it was clear that we weren't going to be picked up. The luxury of being transported back to Manhattan in an air conditioned taxi was beyond our reach. We had the money to pay but we didn't qualify as acceptable looking customers. I had failed to notice at first that the drivers who carried passengers in their back seats were occupied by white customers. The three taxi drivers who I had seen pick up passengers all happened to be white. Was this a coincidence?

Foolishly I was still in denial. I hadn't considered that the colour and tone of our skin would deprive us the privilege of acquiring a cab in this particular area. The speeches and mandates I had absorbed in Britain about equality and diversity had pacified my ability to identify this type of subliminal prejudice.

The failure to secure a taxi wasn't an overtly racist or prejudicial act like being called a derogatory name or told that you have certain negative behavioural traits because you're Black. This was a silent discrimination. To me being ignored in this way was just as painful if not more. A part of me didn't want to shatter my illusion of the progressive American Dream in the Obama era. Subsequently I rejected its truth.

Later on that afternoon we were back mid-town. The subway was our selected method of transport. I had successfully hailed a cab near the hotel. I needed to head downtown to the Soho district and return a pair of shoes I'd purchased from the Steve

Madden store the day before. My brothers opted to stay behind at the hotel because they were exhausted from all the walking around.

Our Manhattan taxi driver was a friendly Haitian man who had migrated to America in 2003. He lived in the Bronx. Despite his daily pickups and regular interactions with tourists from across the world, he was intrigued by my African face and British accent. The Brooklyn cab incident was still bothering me. I shared the encounter with the Haitian driver.

'It's because you're Black' his statement made my heart skip. It was like I'd been punched in my lower stomach without prior warning. I wasn't expecting him to be so blatant about his thoughts. 'When they see you are Black, they think you are going to take them into neighbourhoods like the Bronx or Brooklyn' he said in a softly spoken voice with a hint of a French accent.

'We were already in Brooklyn!' I said defensively. He detected the aggression in my tone and began to stare into his rear view mirror, specifically for the purpose of making eye contact with me. He chuckled before responding.

'The drivers don't want to go to those kinds of neighbourhoods. They prefer to come to Manhattan' he winked. The taxi was ventilating and circulating a cool breeze from its air conditioning system but somehow I was sweating profusely. My temperature was rising along with my temper.

'They shouldn't make assumptions about me, just because I'm Black' I snapped as though the driver were one of the ignorant few who passed me in the sizzling summer heat.

'I was coming to Manhattan anyway. Isn't my money the same colour as anyone else's?' I folded my arms and I slumped further into the leather seat.

My mother remained relaxed as she closed her eyes and fell into a mild sleep. She was calm and unfazed by the incident. On the other hand I'd taken it very personal. This was very naïve of me. How could I believe that I would be immune to the kind of discrimination that African Americans experienced in their own backyards? I had the audacity to think I could avoid it because I was a tourist and born in the UK and I spoke with a British accent. I wasn't from the projects or the so called thug type that society were afraid and suspicious of. How would those drivers have known this?

They were only making judgements upon what they saw. We were two Black Women accompanied by two Black males hailing for a cab on the side walk in Brooklyn. The differentiations of Black which separates us by our geographical location (Black British, African American, African Caribbean or Aboriginal) makes no difference in this type of scenario. By definition our commonality is Black skin and it was the taxi drivers' prerogative not to stop and collect us. That was the discretion they exercised and subsequently abused.

The taxi incident made me remember a song I'd heard in the mid-1990s entitled Invisible by a Black British Boy band called Public Demand. There was a line that always stuck in my head. The handsome brotha croons about trying to hail a taxi which drives right past him. At the time of the singles release Public Demand did an interview as part of a promotional tour and explained this inference. As Black men they found it difficult to pick up taxi's from the streets. In London there are Black cabs (the name refers to the colour of the vehicles) which operate much like the yellow taxi service in New York City. In 1997 I didn't necessarily disbelieve Public Demand's perspective. I simply couldn't identify with it. These men were so accustomed to this behaviour they spoke humorously about it. My first hand taste of this rejection left a bitter taste in my mouth. By no means did I find it funny.

Port Antonio, Jamaica: July 2012

'Cover up ya baby nuh' a petite brown skinned lady adjusted the pink umbrella that was attached to the frame of the pram.

'She gon get Black'. The sun was blazing down at Portland's Jerk Festival and some of the attendees were trying to preserve their complexions. I had watched documentaries about the bleaching epidemic in Jamaica. This was a popular practice in parts of Africa and Asia too. These types of attitudes came as no surprise to me. It's no secret that everywhere there are communities of colour a coded cast system is enforced.

> *The lighter the skin, the more likely to win.*
> *A shade of brown may hold you down.*
> *Being Black can set you back.*

Each day I walked into town I passed a man high up on his ladder that was propped against the house he was repairing. We exchanged pleasantries and without fail he would also remind me of the following.

'Baby you have a nice complexion' he chimed in patois 'don't trouble your colour you hear' he rubbed his fingers against the back of his palm, caressing the skin which was a similar shade to mine. I gave him a thumbs up. I appreciated his reassurance. But my mind was already made up. I was feeling more comfortable about my skin tone. I wouldn't apply any bleach, lemon moisturiser, toner or hydroquinone based product that would compromise the richness of complexion. When people compliment me about my skin tone and tell me it's beautiful I make them aware that I already acknowledge the beauty in myself.

I didn't receive very much attention in Jamaica. My looks weren't so unique. I saw a number of people who resembled Ghanaians like myself and my family in Africa. The island was strikingly similar to Ghana. The way it smelt and the green landscape. If I had been blindfolded and abandoned in the country I would have believed that I was back home. Ghana and Jamaica are like two siblings who bare a very strong resemblance.

Visiting the Island was quite a bitter sweet experience. I thought back to my childhood days when West Indian and West African children were divided by their belief that one was superior to the other. Had we all been blessed with the opportunity to visit one another's countries of origin we would have been educated on how our heritage was interlinked.

Looking back in history it seems that the rivalry between Black people from the Caribbean and Africa happened when we migrated to Britain. This was the first time we lived in close proximity to one another. From what I've heard and read I've come to understand that we didn't respect one another's differences and acknowledge the elements of our cultures that could bind us together as we fought against prejudice and racism.

We could have continued to retain our cultures and sense of ethnic pride by uniting because we should have understood that racially we are part of a much larger social group as Black people.

In my teenage years I had a conversation with a St Lucian class mate about this.

'Do you realise that I have more in common with you then I do with a person who was born and raised in Ghana?. We've got a shared identity as Black Britons' I sincerely believed this and still do for that matter. Black British people form their own group as we can contextualise our experience of living as people of colour in the United Kingdom. A step towards strengthening the Black community is by embracing this concept. We must recognise that we are one unified collective. It doesn't matter if we were born in Nigeria or our parents are of Guyanese descent. We can still tap into these cultures whole heartedly. Many Black Britons have settle in the UK for more than an entire generation. Regardless of whether we are Christians, Jewish, Muslim, Buddhists, Black Israelites or atheists, our religious beliefs may differ yet we are of the same race. There are issues relating to poor housing, education, high unemployment, high crime, economic deprivation that exist in the Black community. These are universal issues that occur in Black neighbourhoods across the globe. We can't work towards solving any of these issues if we aren't moving in the same direction.

Conversations of Colour: 2012

Boss lady

Linda aka Boss Lady and I were sitting at our desks in the open plan office as we often did. One of the senior managers walked past our seating area in order to return to his teams seating section. He greeted us both. Linda exchanged his pleasantries with a melodic hello and a wide smile. From the corner of my eyes I saw her double take .

'Clive have you been swimming in gravy' she broke into a fit of laughter. I didn't share her sense of humour. I noticed that she was looking at me to capture my reaction. For this reason alone my eyes remained fixed upon my computer screen. I didn't want to entertain this level of stupidity. The senior manager had clearly obtained a tan from a short holiday break. I couldn't understand why she made the link between his tanned complexion and gravy? I didn't think it was complimentary or funny.

There was another instance. We were in a team meeting and Linda was desperately trying to describe a male colleague from our department.

'The tall man, with the pineapple' Linda raised her hands upon her head and gestured as though she were imitating the top of a pineapple with its green spiked leaves. Her fingers extended outwards. I must admit that I giggled. Not because I found her impersonation funny. I thought it was a ridiculous way to describe a Black man with dreadlocks worn up in a ponytail. Once again she was trying to be sarcastic and I thought she was actually being pathetic.

Then there was the story of a young man she had once taught. She happened to bump into him outside our office one evening. She told me a story about how he had once called her a bitch.

'What a coincidence that he happens to work close by' she smirked 'you must have seen him outside. He is a Negro but he's albino' she added.

A Negro? I wondered. What a strange phrase to use when referring to a Black person in this day and age. In all honesty (with the exception of films and documentaries) I'd never seen a white person refer to someone of African descent as a Negro! Not in the 2000s. Nobody had ever said this word in my presence. I very rarely heard Black people use the term. The word is a phrase that is avoided because it sounds very much like Nigger. I considered that she was going to say the word Nigger (by mistake) but promptly used the term Negro to supplement it.

Manhattan : July 2013

I sat at the dining table of the Holiday Inn eating breakfast alone. A tall light skinned man in his mid-40s walked past my table in the opposite direction and headed for the vending machine. He was chatting away on his mobile phone loud enough for all of the diners to hear. He walked confidently with his shoulders and chest held high. I thought his choice of attire which consisted of an oversized football jersey, denim three quarter length shorts and Nike trainers was a little bit too young for him.

I noticed that he grabbed some food from the buffet area and proceeded back towards his seating section. We caught eyes for a brief moment. His large palms cupped his tiny mobile phone that was pressed against his ear.

'You are so Black' his voice echoed. I didn't get the opportunity to react before he made his next comment

'You're beautiful' his voice seemed to be getting louder.

'Yo! I'm on the phone here' he laughed and pointed towards the handset.

'She's beautiful man' he said to his friend on the other side of the line.

'Thank you' I replied not really knowing what else I was expected to say in response.

I didn't feel embarrassed I appreciated his admiration for Black beauty. When your looks have been ridiculed and marginalised by the media for as long as you can remember it's nice for people to let you know that they recognise your worth even if it doesn't happen very often.

Buying make-up in New York was like a ritual for me. I enjoyed seeing the glamorous people at the cosmetics counters. The brands sold a much wider variety of colours. This time I wanted to sample the best of what Urban Decay had to offer. I was equipped with the list I had conjured up after watching make-up tutorials online.

A handsome young Latino looking man assisted me. He wanted to experiment with every colour that he swore would suit my complexion.

'You're beautiful' he told me and I thanked him but was cautious because he was a sales rep whose aim was to make me part with my cash. One of his colleagues, a beautiful light skinned Black lady was also on hand to help me find the right shades of eye shadows. After 30 minutes I had made my choice and paid.

'Isn't she beautiful?' the friendly assistant said to his colleague.

'Where are you from?' she chimed and I proudly replied Ghana.

'That's why. You're so exotic'.

I stared at them suspiciously before expressing my thanks. I wanted to detect whether they were lying to me, but why would they? They didn't owe me anything. I took the compliment and tried not to read into things so much because at the end of the day the most important thing was feeling happy about myself. Finally I felt that being Black was enough I could finally embrace my blackness whole heartedly.

London: July 2013

Sareena and I had used the toilet and were waiting for Janette so we could walk back to the Overground station together. Moments before I had apologised to a secretary in an nearby office. A petite and pretty Southern Asian young lady. We needed to get the code to gain access to the toilet cubicle. The secretary was kind enough to unlock the door for us as we'd politely requested. Within two minutes a slim white middle aged lady with short brown hair (wearing a black trouser suit) emerged from the very same office where we could hear the secretary typing away.

'Hello. What's the problem?' she asked in a stern voice as she cupped her small palms together. She stared at us.

'Hello' I replied. I wondered who this lady was and why her energy was so static. She seemed very tense. Her choice of the word 'problem' was indicative of her negative temperament.

'There's is no problem we were trying to use these toilets and couldn't get in. We are waiting for our colleague who is still inside'.

'Who are you here to see?' she asked firmly.

'We are exam invigilators' I said as I could anticipate what the woman's next request would be. I still couldn't figure out who she was. Predictably she requested that we vacate the area and wait for our friend in the main reception. She even took the trouble of escorting us out to the main entrance of the school. As we paced along the corridor she introduced herself to us.

'I'm the head teacher' she also mentioned her name but I couldn't remember it. My heart sank as she identified herself. I was surprised by her conduct and that she had the time to patrol the schools hallway outside her office.

'Okay' Sareena replied she may have been just as surprised as I. Sareena had a teenage daughter. Perhaps she was used to dealing with teachers. She remained as calm and collected..

'How have you found the school?' the head mistress questioned in a flat tone which showed me that she was engaging us in small talk so the walk towards the entrance wasn't silent and awkward.

'Have you enjoyed it?'

'Yes very much so' I lied.

'Yes it's been really good' Sareena added. I tried to maintain my composure because I didn't want to give her the satisfaction of knowing that we were offended by her approach. She bid us goodbye and returned back through the secured doors in the direction of her office. Sareena and I remained seated in the reception area until Janette joined us.

I was truly taken aback by how rude and confrontational the head teacher seemed to be. Engaging us in a conversation as she walked us out was insulting. Her conduct reminded me of the mannerisms that some of my teachers had when I was at school. At times they were quite condescending and patronising. Maybe she thought we were on work experience? Sareena was almost 40 years old but looked half her age. However we were wearing our day badges to identify that we were legitimate visitors to the school. We had been working there for a month by this time. All she had to do was ask us to keep the noise down as we waited. The fact that she walked us out of the school was beyond me. We were going to leave in a few minutes anyway. I appreciate that she had a duty of care and school staff are responsible for safeguarding their pupils. But we were not strangers. The head mistress was the feistiest person I'd met in years. In the weeks we'd spent working at the school those were the toilets we'd been using. So what was her problem that day? If she didn't want us to use this toilet then all she had to do was say so.

'You see how they speak to you like you're a pickney' Sareena moaned in patois as kissed her teeth. She clearly felt the same way I did.

'She's so rude!' I shook my head 'we could have been anyone waiting there'. However when the head teacher established that we weren't anybody particularly senior or important she steered us out.

Why did she ask if there was a 'problem' first and foremost? We weren't causing any trouble. That was a rhetorical question on her part. I knew what the head teacher's problem was she was using her superiority to belittle us. This is what is known in Britain as 'pulling rank or to pull rank'. If she wanted us to vacate the area and told us we would have done so without resistance. Instead she escorted us out like we were intruders and she a security guard. I think she should have introduced herself to us in the first instance. She could have said Hi my name is Mrs ABC, I'm the head teacher. Is everything okay? Can I help you ladies? Like any other person with manners would. My point is she didn't have the common courtesy to do this. Her approach would have altered depending on who she thought she was dealing with. She was a horrible woman. I've been around long enough to know how people are based on my first few minutes of meeting them. Thankfully this was one of our final days at her school.

Sareena had made her way home via the Overground station. Janette and I walked towards train station. I continued to discuss the incident with Janette.

'You know what that was all about?' Janette took a brief pause and lit a cigarette between her bony fingers. She inhaled and exhaled a ball of smoke.

'She saw a group of young Black girls in the corridor and thought we were up to no good'

'You think?' I said sarcastically.

'Yeah, course man' Janette rolled her eyes.

Janette's reaction was quite surprising to me. The first day we'd (met prior to this incident beside the toilet) Janette had asked me to guess what her racial background was. She had dark wavy afro type hair with kinky roots. Her eyes were dark and her skin a light shade of brown with caramel under tones. Janette had full lips and a broad button nose. I thought she was Black with a little bit of European and Indian ancestry in her family just like millions of people whose parents hail from the Caribbean Islands or Afro South Americans.

'My mum's Persian and my dad's Jamaican' she smiled.

'Okay' what else could I say? I thought she was Guyanese at most. Janette had shared stories about growing about in an abusive environment. At the time she was in a relationship with a handsome young Irish man this was a volatile situation as she claimed he would often beat her. At 23 years old Janette had already been through so much.

Janette took pride in promoting her racial identity nonetheless she recognised how she was perceived by the head teacher under these circumstances. She acknowledged that she was just as Black as Sareena and I.

Visibly Invisible: South-East London: July 2014

I lay in my bed in darkness. The sound of laughter and music had disturbed me from my sleep. My bedroom window remained open to allow air to circulate around the humid room. After a short while I found myself singing along to the lyrics of Pharelle's tune Happy, Blurred Lines by Robin Thicke and Beyoncé's anthem Single Ladies. The music echoed from the garden of a house nearby. I heard the party goers singing. Their renditions of the popular tunes were out of sync and off pitch. I could only imagine how terrible their dance coordination skills were.

Whilst writing these monologues my mind analysed everything I was seeing in the context of race. I thought about how influential African and Caribbean culture had been upon contemporary pop music, fashion, beauty and politics. Then I heard the baseline of Jamaican Dancehall artist Beenie Man's no.1 hit Who am I? The party guests were only able to sing along to the chorus. Beenie's patois speaking verses were too complex for them to understand and imitate. They weren't discouraged. Just as long as there was a beat that they could try and dance to. I thought about the irony of the moment. They were playing Black music. I glanced through the window and gazed into the neighbour's garden. There wasn't a single Black face amongst the crowd. Just like certain aspects of the entertainment industry. Black people are visible and invisible at the same time.

The True Beauty of Blackness: Summer 2014

I've taught myself a valuable lesson. I don't resemble the majority of Black women in the beauty magazines or on television. My looks don't conform to the westernised standards of beauty. My nose is big, my eyes are wide and dark. My hair is short and tightly coiled. My skin is the darkest shade of brown, at times it appears Black.

I am beautiful. Why? I see beauty when I look in the mirror. I'm not searching for it on television or anywhere else in the biased media. I don't tap into these outlets in search of my identity or to validate what I already know This positive reinforcement and love for my own heritage isn't a rejection or criticism of any other race. Why should it be?

I sincerely hope that a girl who looks like me. A young and impressionable Rose whose perception of self has been defined by those around her. A female who doesn't believe she is attractive because she doesn't meet the westernised standards of beauty can feel the same way I do.

There are times I feel discouraged. Even today, at a stage where I believe I have counselled myself and healed. I get annoyed because there are people who aren't that attractive who somehow believe that they are superior to people who look like me because they have less pigment in their skin. I've told myself that I have the right to believe I am great too. If they can be mean spirited and beautiful. Even when their personalities suggest the opposite.

I don't mind being seen. I'm no longer hiding behind my black clothing, hoping to blend in and be ignored by society. In fact I enjoy wearing white. I absorb the compliments from people who tell me that I look radiant in ivory because it suits my Black complexion. I hold on to the praise at times because it gives me a sense of meaning and purpose. I have to focus on something positive. However, I am still suspicious when I visit a makeup counter and the beautician tells me that ravishing red shade and bright orange complements my skin tone. I know my limitations.

As for the Images of beauty and the belief systems that perpetuate these portrayals. European features are upheld as the ideal and Black African characteristics are side-lined. I realise that it takes a very smart person to see the beauty of dark skinned women like myself. They have to decode the messages and unravel the disparaging remarks that condemned the representations of Black skin in the mainstream. If one can recognise and appreciate Black beauty amidst all the hype and discouragement its truly is inspiring.

Binary Blackness

There isn't a single word, sentence or paragraph that can summarise the concept of blackness in all of its complexity. The multiple definitions and interpretations of blackness composed by everyday people and academics alike, are as varied as the skin tones that it represents. We are more than the melanin we possess. Skin isn't just scientific and biological. There are social and spiritual dimensions that exist to exemplify its meaning. The more I learn about the history of people of colour, the greater my understanding becomes of our relationships with other ethnic groups (particularly the Europeans and other Black people worldwide). Everything I knew or wasn't sure about when it came to race related matters seems to make a lot more sense as time goes by.

Within our separate racial categorisations there are stereotypes and misconceptions we have about one another. Many of which have existed prior to the prevalence of slavery. These prejudices and beliefs have remained in the realm of human consciousness for so long that it is difficult to establish how they came to be. One thing that becomes apparent. The racial systems as we know them in present day society as it has evolved over time are reflective of societies changing attitudes.

Dr Frances Cress Welsing (African American psychiatrist and writer of The Isis Papers: The Keys to Colors, 1991) states that the hierarchical structure created by the prevalence of governing (white supremacy) exists in all areas of human activity. Welsing refers to following key areas:

- Media/Entertainment
- Religion
- Politics/Governance
- Sex
- Law Enforcement
- Entertainment
- Economics.

Cress Welsing argues that in spite of the oppressive effects that the white supremacist social structure has upon people of colour, Black people can still excel and function. However Welsing reinforces how fundamental it is to recognise racism. If people of colour are unable to identify and understand the system of white supremacy then everything else they experience in the world will confuse them. Welsing like many other African American scholars recommends that individuals draw up their own definitions of white supremacy.

For the purpose of writing the Melanin Monologues I thought it would be appropriate to explore and construct my own definition of white supremacy.

White Supremacy

White Supremacy is about dominance and denial. The self- proclaimed need for the ruling classes to dominate those who they regard as inferior (Blacks/people of colour) by way of their physical appearance and cultural practices. This is measured against concepts of whiteness and the idea that whiteness translates to a natural state of being, a cultural norm which other racial groups must adhere to or aspire to attain. In dominating, the elite can effectively retain and maintain economic, political, religious and social ownership over subordinate groups in the best interest of their own social structures.

A white supremacist mind set promotes the notion (historically) that only those who are part of the white ruling elite class have the authority and resources to define whiteness and officially categorise who belongs to specific racial groups. In this respect whiteness is exclusive and divisional. Physical attributes held by people of colour (such as dark skin, course hair or characteristically African facial features are used to distinguish people of colour from those who regard themselves as white. This is best demonstrated by the one drop rule where slave owners in the US stated that if anyone had one drop of Black , Asian or Native Indian blood in their gene pool they were considered to be Black or a person of colour and not white.

White supremacy is about Power. The power for the white population to arrive in every area of the globe, whether it be habitable or vacant. Ownership is taken of these regions regardless of who the indigenous folk are or how long they have occupied the space in the absence of western practices and customs of living. This has happened historically for example the transatlantic slave trade, the European invasion in Tasmania (Australia) and imperialism in India. The power to conquer and enforce is not isolated to property, it extends to and permeates every aspect of human activity as Welsing discusses.

To enforce such practices there has to be some element of denial as there is resistance from the oppressed subjects. Their protests must be eliminated in place of the belief that their interference operates in the best interest of those who are to be transformed. Psychiatrists like Welsing have argued that white supremacist/racist views is a form of mental illness, which involves the hallucinating denial of whiteness by Europeans. A failure to acknowledge a position of power and superiority over other racial groups.

White Supremacy illuminates white confidence. The confidence to interject a white belief system as the most progressive line of thought. The belief that the white way, is the right way. Irrespective of what any other race of people in the entire world believe.

Dr William Lez Henry author of Whiteness Made Simple (2007) emphasises that Black people are the 'best witnesses to whiteness, because white folk don't seem to get what is at stake when merely trying to 'live' whilst being Black in their world' (p.13). Their world most likely refers to the white space they occupy within their own communities and internationally. For the dominant, ruling groups and the subjects who have been afforded the privilege of assimilation into the realm of whiteness "it is natural to be white; it is natural for them to be white and oppress blacks (p.13).

Robert Knox (author of Races of Men, 1850) held the belief that was an important factor of civilizations. He concluded that Blacks cannot be civilized. His research was unfavourable towards Blacks. The racist and prejudicial sentiment of his views of 'the dark races' were shared and held by the ruling elites of his time. To some degree it provides an understanding of why it was necessary for the dominant group to retain power in their historical pro-segregation and racist perspectives.

In the belief that Black people were physically and mentally inferior to other races Knox's analogy was used to justify why Blacks could provide work force labour.

Know spoke of the regions across the world such as 'the Indian empire' that provided a substantial amount of money Britain. The Central African districts presently known as The Democratic republic of Congo was wealthy due to its productive soil. Knox was discussed how regrettable it was that colonial officials were unable to tolerate the climate condition during the Europeans earliest attempts of trying to take over the country.

Knox elaborated upon how the indigenous people were regarded as a 'feeble Black population' who by way of nature occupied a geographical region with potential wealth. The so called dark races of Central Africa would have been used for labour force much like the natives in Indian without any negotiation. The fact that they were inferior justified the forcible takeover of their lands. The Europeans were relentless in their pursuit of such territories and the indigenous people had to accept their fate as slaves or being annihilated.

Racial Reality: Mental Health

I have looked into the works of psychiatrist Dr Umar Johnson in addition to Welsing. to consider how relevant it is from a Black British perspective. In their discussions relating to the mental wellbeing of Black patients each has explored the idea that Black people suffer from mental health issues in response to white supremacy. When I read this claim I became very defensive. But I had to admit I was hurting too. Dr Johnson summarised this as Black people's tendency to hate what they are and love what they can never be! I wondered. Was I one of those who held such a tragic belief? I hoped not yet I had to be honest with myself. Maybe I didn't hate myself but I certainly resented my blackness at times. My blackness had exposed me and denied me of elevating to a higher social status. As Black people a substantial amount of us are conditioned to believe that there is a glass ceiling that rests above the heads. One of which was impenetrable and would prevent us from social and economic mobility. I believed it because over the years I had been told that I could never be pretty or successful because of my blackness in a western society. There were places that I would never be accepted because people would judge me before I spoke. I was inferior because of my blackness. I didn't necessary want to look or be white. I don't think most black people do. But there is a yearning to be afforded the luxury of access to white opportunities. A desire to possess the keys and hold the answers that can only be obtained through whiteness.

As a Black British woman I knew I would be stereotyped and that people could only view me through a preconceived notion and image that has been projected by the media before Black people even arrived on western shores. There are stereotypes that we had no say in constructing and ones that we can never change. No matter what we do or how we try. When I think about of Black women in the public eye, the reoccurring images spring to mind:

- A sexually promiscuous Amazonian, exotic harlot. An insatiable whore who's body is subjected to rape and ridicule.

- The Black woman as a pacified, a sexual, domesticated mammy type. Eager to please and ready to clean.

- The notion of a single, loud mouthed angry Black woman. Who is constantly ready to fight.

- The Babymama (US)/ Babymother (UK) who is raising her children alone. Each baby belonging to a different father.

I struggled to identify with anyone of these groups. However these were images that had been presented before my eyes as a young and impressionable child. There were some, but very view.

When I reflect upon the juxtaposition of the concepts of whiteness and blackness my mind trailed back to an evening I sat in a Library in Lambeth (South London) at the film club. I went to watch the screening of a film called Rabbit Proof Fence (2002). The viewing gave me some insight into the Black experience from an Aboriginal perspective. Set in the 1930s, the Australian government implements a policy where they forcibly remove mixed race children of Aboriginal/European descent from the rural areas where they lived with their maternal (Aboriginal) family members. The aim of this procedure was to 'breed the Blackness out of the country'. These children are known as Australia's stolen generation. Some of them were never reunited with their biological family members. These children were taken to children's homes where they were later educated, taught about Christianity and sent to live with white families in a bid to make them assimilate into white culture. The film is based upon three little girls mixed race girls who met the same fate. The story was indicative of what was happening in a wider context as this was occurring all over the country.

Of course I was saddened by the film. But I didn't cry like the middle aged white lady who sobbed uncontrollably in the seat beside me. I thought about the concept of white supremacy and considered how it influenced her reaction. These tears were triggered by the deeply rooted white guilt she felt. I glanced at her from the corner of my eye. I couldn't feel as sympathetic towards her emotional outbreak as I would have done years before.

Like many other Black people I (during childhood and adult years) had watched numerous films that told the stories of Africans removed from the comfort of their homelands to be beaten, stripped of their clothing as well as their culture and raped. I had wept when I watched films and read stories about the South African apartheid system, a regime that continued to be enforced as recently as the 1990s. Watching the film based upon the racist murder of Stephen Lawrence in Eltham, South London was also very difficult. My tears were shed for those Black people. They could have been me or a close relative. Time and distance saved us from these traumatic circumstances. The sweet middle aged lady had the privilege of watching the enforcement of a racist power structure from a far.

When the films credits rolled the damsel in distress commented on what a moving story it was. She wiped her tears and I imaged that she would retire to her nearby terraced home where her husband and family were probably safely tucked away in bed. Perhaps my feelings were triggered by my understanding that beyond the TV screen, the effects of racial oppression would never be a part of her existence.

Friend

You've been there for me,

Whenever I have called.

Through the good times and the bad,

You've stood by me through it all.

When I needed somebody,

To wipe my tears away.

You listened and brought comfort.

You uplifted me each day.

To a very special friend,

Who means so very much,

Your kindness is immeasurable.

You warm every heart you touch.

Ebony and Ivory

Rachel and I entered Greenwich Park after we'd eaten at a local pizzeria

'You smell like chocolate' Rachel sniffed the skin of my right arm. We both laughed. Our conversations always seemed to digress onto the subject of race.

'It's psychological' I replied.

'You always smell like chocolate Nat' Rachel said.

'Black people always use skin moisturizers and hair pomades that have a fruity smell. That's what you're smelling!' I explained. Rachel frowned. She wasn't entirely convinced.

Through the course of our eleven year friendship we would engage ourselves in the most interesting topics about race. I found Rachel to be a lot more open than other white people I'd discussed such issues with. She wasn't afraid to ask me questions or admit that she didn't know something that she would be expected to understand about people of colour (because she grew up in a multi-cultural environment).

Rachel didn't make assumptions or stereotype as quickly as others would. Nor did she jump on the bandwagon of lazy generalisations often made by ignorant people in reference to things they had little or no knowledge about. Rachel put her trust in me and I would answer any queries she had with patience and honesty. In turn she extended me the same courtesy.

Rachel wasn't aware that I was writing the Melanin Monologues. It came as perfect timing when she called me on one of my days off . I was in the process of developing a chapter. She informed me that that she would be visiting London (as she did twice a year since before she left the city to set up home with her fiancé). Her timing (for making contact with me) was very convenient and she had a question for me. This was the scenario.

Rachel had a friend who I will refer to as Donna. Donna's mother is white and her father mixed raced (one black parent and one white parent). Donna was about to have a baby with a white British man.

'What colour will that make her baby?' Rachel queried.

'Well your friend isn't white Rachel. She may look it but she isn't'.

I then explained to Rachel that this could be answered in a social and scientific capacity. Socially, it may be convenient for the baby to be identified as white as the baby will most likely look European. This causes less confusion. The family will not have to explain how the baby is mixed when the baby's entire immediate family appear white. In addition the baby may well be thought of as white because it has a higher percentage of European blood more so than Black.

Then there is the scientific concept. Biologically the child has Black ancestry in his or her gene pool, regardless of how European the baby might look. Therefore the baby couldn't be white. I explained that Black genes are dominant so the family could have an African looking child born to them in later years. Particularly if there is Black heritage in both Donna and her partner's DNA. The Black characteristics (hair, skin tone, features) could resurface without prior warning. This is known as a 'throw back'.

'Your friend's baby could end up looking darker than your friend or her mixed raced father. With genes it could either anyway' I added. History has a tendency to repeat itself and the manifestation of colour in a white family is no exception to that rule.

'What colour does your friend identify herself as?' I asked Rachel out of curiosity and reminded her that this perception would influence how Donna would choose to racially categorise her own child. If she thought of herself as mixed raced she may extend this to her child's ethnic classification.

'That's a good question. I'm not sure' Rachel said.

'I bet it's white' I said knowing that this would also depend upon how white Donna looked. This wouldn't necessarily mean that Donna is ashamed of her Black ancestry. She would perhaps choose to be identified as white for the purpose of assimilation and because it most accurately describes her outward physical appearance. In a social capacity, if being Black is considered somewhat of a socially progressive hindrance and white equates to power and privilege then why wouldn't she tap into it if she could?

Rachel said she was going to find out what Donna's thoughts were about her own racial identity. However Rachel claimed that by looking at Donna it was obvious that her friend was a person of colour. Rachel therefore wasn't sure that Donna opting to be white or defining herself as 'white other' was a plausible description of her ethnicity.

'What do you see?' I asked Rachel as she was the first white person I had heard acknowledge that they could tell whether someone had Black blood in their genes especially if the person looked European. Alternatively I know of many Black people (including myself) who are able to tell/detect the slightest amount of colour in a person.

'It's something about her freckles, the darkness of her eyes and the structure of her face. She has a really athletic build and she has got quite a broad frame and big calves'. We both laughed at Rachel's detailed observation, yet I knew what she meant. These are the type of characteristics that people of colour are able to spot in those who are white yet have other racial ancestry within their backgrounds.

Donna's story reminded me of a woman who I used to work with. She had slightly tanned skin, blue eyes and straight brown her. Nicola's father was white British and her mother South African, Cape Coast Coloured (mixed with African, Asian and a small percentage of European ancestry). Nicola was married to an Italian man.

'I tick white other' Nicola had once confirmed when I asked her how she specified her racial background on application forms.

'Because I don't want to deny my mother' Nicola added. I thought this was quite ironic. Nicola perceived 'white other' to be a category that best explained her race and to acknowledge her mother's heritage. From a social perception I understood this option. Nicola could be regarded as 'white other' without raising any further questions or doubts. If her mother was a person of colour with mainly Black and Asian ancestry then the 'mixed other' or 'other ethnic background' categories would have been a more viable option. Doesn't white + colour (be it Black, Asian, Latino or mixed) equate to being a person of mixed heritage?

There have been many debates I have witnessed and been involved with about the complexities of colour categorisation. A young lady I went to school with who was born to a white British mother and Kenyan/Ugandan father had agitated her father as she was filling in application forms to apply for college. She selected the 'mixed – white & Black African' option on her form. Her father resented this and was adamant that she should select 'Black African' as her racial group. I never learned why he felt so strongly about that. Sure enough she did look Black. More so light skinned. My class mates and I were amazed to see that she had a white mother when we had our very first parents evening at school.

Evidently there aren't any clearly defined guidelines when it comes to race. It may come as no surprise to learn that it varies depending on the environment we are in and how we are socialised. In the time I spent working in the library service after I left university I observed how people identified themselves racially when they completed application forms to join the service. This was one of the most interesting parts of the job. I noticed a trend. People with fair to olive complexions had a tendency to identify themselves as 'white other' these were Turkish, Italian, Greek, Spanish, North African people –in addition to others from the Mediterranean region. I have seen people who are considered to be Arabs tick other racial background or occasionally opt for 'white other'.

I once came across a woman who had light skin and afro hair she may have had a mixed raced parent, however she opted for the 'White British' choice. I had also seen a woman who appeared to be Black with a medium brown complexion tick 'mixed'. She had chosen to identify her son (who was visibly Black) as mixed raced. I try not to judge someone based on their colour because it's difficult to give a definitive answer on what their racial background is. Sometimes you really can't tell!

At the time of writing the Melanin Monologues my friend Rachel was engaged to a young man called Anthony. They were living in the town where he'd grown up. There were very few people of colour based there. I found it quite comforting when Rachel told me she had befriended an East African lady who was the only Black person in her work environment.

'Are you trying to find someone like me?' I joked. She said she just gravitated towards this young lady who happened to be very nice. Her friendship with this particular colleague reminded me of how we had first got talking when we met at Sixth Form College. Rachel said that I reminded her of a friend she had met at secondary school who she was very close to. Perhaps she felt that there is something about Black women that she relates too which makes her able to establish great friendships with us.

Rachel would often educate Anthony about people of colour. Naturally because he hadn't really socialised with Black people in his own community (there were hardly any) his views were shaped by the media's portrayal. At times this led to inaccurate assumptions and stereotyping. For example Rachel told me that she had to explain to Anthony that Chris Brown and Rhianna were not 'half white'. Anthony believed they were because of their light skinned complexions. Rachel told him that Black people ranged in complexions and there were people in the Black community who had darker skin than the two (Brown and Rhianna) yet one white parent. This sounds so simple but the fact is if people don't learn about other people's history and culture. The simplest things can become complicated or misinterpreted.

Coffee and Cream: Autumn 2013

Rachel and I sat in a coffee shop at the local shopping mall. More than a year had passed by since we'd last seen each other. I gave the spillage about my disastrous dating experiences and the challenges I was facing at work. Rachel updated me about her employment status and relationship. During our previous meeting she told me that she was engaged and I wanted to find out whether she was closer to securing a wedding date.

Rachel asked me how I would feel about being a bridesmaid at her wedding. I joked about being the only Black person in the entire town. I knew this might well be the case. Nevertheless I wanted to be a part of the wedding if my best friend wanted and needed me there. The fact she took the time out to ask me how I would feel gave an indication of her compassionate character. She finds a way to understand the Black experience especially if it is one that affects the life of a close friend. For this reason I could take pride in calling Rachel one of my best friends.

I can't remember what led me to begin defining to Rachel what it felt like to be a Black woman in 2013.

'Being Black is something I think about every day. Something always happens to remind me that I'm Black' Rachel's eyebrows raised into a frown. Her face transformed into a shade of red, she looked horrified.

'It's funny because I can't imagine thinking about being white every day. I don't even think about it' she stated.

'The things is' I took a sip from my cappuccino 'we live in one world but different worlds at the same time. That's because what we see and how we are treated makes our view of life different' Rachel remained silent as I went onto explain.

'You don't have to think about your whiteness because you never have to. It doesn't present any challenges. Your colour isn't promoted as being different! You look like the people on TV, magazines and those who are running the country' I said as I noticed Rachel's lip quiver. I anticipated what her next comment would be so I continued.

'When I say look like you I mean you are the same colour as the people who have the most power and influential positions in this society' she nodded in response to my theory. We both agreed that it was quite strange but we were given some insight into one another's reality. Truthfully speaking our friendship existed in the realms of two dimensions. A white aspect and a Black. To find common ground and speak honestly with one another we had to be open minded and empathise with our individual perceptions of race. If we didn't then we couldn't communicate on this level.

Rachel took my views quite seriously. I remember one particular occasion I strongly suggested that she remove a comment from her Facebook page. She compared the spices she'd grown in her home to the smell of an 'Indian brothel'. Although I wasn't clear of what she meant I took into consideration that she couldn't equate the smell of her spices to an environment in a country she'd never visited. I sincerely believe that it was not her intention to be offensive. She respected my opinion enough to remove her comment and she was very apologetic.

Black Face, White Space

I came across a documentary entitled Whitewashed: Unmasking the World of Whiteness (2013) that explored the concept of whiteness (there are plenty of debates and studies written about race). The documentary was particularly insightful. The white participants spoke candidly about their own perspectives of whiteness. I am under the impression that they were being interviewed by a white researcher which facilitated their ability to speak earnestly about the subject.

The interviewees were American's who are descendants of white settlers who migrated to the US from all corners of Europe. The vast majority of participants declared that they have never been challenged to think consciously about their whiteness. This is primarily because their colour has posed no obvious threat or visible obstacle to their lives. In turn the need to address their whiteness hadn't ever arisen. On the other hand for me and most likely a substantial amount of Blacks and people of colour it's the total opposite. As previously mentioned I am highly conscious of being Black. Whether I choose not to remember my race there are external influences that constantly remind me of my skin colour. Blackness virtually becomes an obsession. Why? In a westernised society I have been conditioned to factor my blackness into every decision I make. I have been brought up post-civil rights movement. In the UK my generation inherited a race relations system that came after the 1976 Race Relations act which was enforced to further enhance equality for so called minorities. I am constantly reminded and somewhat pressurised to declare my blackness. Even when I told that I live in a society where it no longer matters.

When I fill out an application form I must specify my race (as others do). When I go to work in an office there are unofficial universal codes that I recognise as a person of colour. You may not agree. Especially if you're not a Black person. You perhaps wouldn't understand or recognise it because you have never been faced with the same need to alter the characteristics and attributes that come to you intrinsically and are part of your cultural heritage.

Take my hair for example which is kinky in its natural state. In a corporate working environment (without being told by anyone) I recognise that I would be expected not to wear my hair in a big afro hair style. Why? The majority of my colleagues are most likely to be white, so I would automatically be different. If there were Black people it is unlikely they would wear their hair in such a way. If you disagree then observe for yourself. When was the last time you saw someone with a big natural afro working in a corporate environment? What about sporting dreadlocks? Have you witnessed this? If you have then I bet it doesn't happened very often.

I would be expected to tame this element of my blackness by perhaps straightening my hair or weaving weaved in hair extensions. As long as it wasn't a natural hairstyle that is too ethnic such as a great big afro. My skin complexion constitutes as being my signal of blackness. That would be more than enough in a professional environment without having a militant hair do to match. How do I know this? A great deal of our conditioning and secondary socialisation comes from the media. On television how many people do you see who are Black working in a corporate environment (whether it's a documentary or TV programme) and wearing an afro? How many staff or managers or executives? You see we learn and absorb these messages as children.

Of course professional and responsible people of all races are conscious of their appearance and attitude. Particularly in their working environment or when they are trying to make a good impression. On a personal level I have to think very carefully about how I present myself in terms of the way I walk, talk, dress and behave. There are stereotypes of Black women that have been perpetuated and circulated but not essentially created by Black people. My behaviour like several other Black people is often judged and measured against these misconceptions. There is a legacy of typical Black female traits that I must be conscious of in every environment I find myself in. I have tried my best not to adhere to these. Television and the media is the most prominent place where these stereotypes are enacted and reinforced. Yes, you can argue that there are negative characters and representations of people of all races in the media. HOWEVER (and I am sure people would agree) amongst Europeans a greater balance prevails.

You can watch TV and see depictions of white people acting badly yet there are enough images of white people (politicians, super models, high profile actress) in positions of power and positively presented to counter act and create an equilibrium. Unfortunately this can't be said for Blacks per se. I don't think it's enough to justify the presence of an African American president as claim that Black people are now viewed positively in the media as people tend to do. Nevertheless it's a step forward.

I can proudly say that when I was a little girl I had the pleasure of seeing Moira Stewart, Zeinab Badawi, Rianna Scipio, Jacqui Harper and Gillian Joseph, later followed by Ronke Phillips reading the news on terrestrial British TV. This was in the days before cable and Sky television networks were available in many UK households. In the 1990s ethnic minority broadcasting became more popular and independent channels were being launched on subscription TV service.

These sistas were truly inspirational and made their mark as strong presenters in a predominately white and male industry.

I once remember seeing Gillian Joseph on daytime TV with braided hair extensions. Initially I was quite surprised. I later watched a documentary (I don't recall the subject) Gillian talked about her decision to change her hairstyle by wearing braids. She joked about her manager implying that the style was a little 'too ethnic'.

Back to my original point about the self-awareness and recognition of race. A lady in the documentary about whiteness phrased it quite eloquently. Her ability to not be challenged or pressurised into acknowledging her white British ancestry (as an American) lies in the fact that she didn't need to think about her whiteness. Racial issues which may be a constant hindrance for other ethnic groups do not present her with the same challenges. In turn this leaves that space in her mind free so that she can think about other things.

Henry (2007) articulates a similar idea:

"White people do not really have to consider how their whiteness is an ever- present non- presence that moulds and shapes a lived reality; which bestows 'gifts', 'benefits' and 'privileges' upon them that have to be 'earned', in one way or another, by Black people' (p.39). Race permeates all areas of society. The blatant exploitation of slaves by their owners and overt racist views is not as obvious today as it had once been. However the current white supremacist structure we have inherited from this legacy remains. There are remnants of the objectives of slavery today. Not to mention the economic wealth inherited by the descendants of slave masters. The wealth and power structure has been retained within European/white possession.

The methods have changed for obtaining and sustaining these goals. But the aims remain the same. A denial of this system, the dismissal of slavery, inequality and exploitation as a thing that happened years ago facilitates and fuels the white supremacist hierarchical power. Before inequality can be tackled it must be diagnosed. The failure and refusal to acknowledge radical imbalance can be subconscious (it has been happening for so many years that people of all races believe it's normal and intrinsic to the human race). Or it can very intentional. For those in power who may not want the system to change as they are able to function and navigate through society without restraint. Hence they are appropriating its denial.

Angry Black Woman (A Tribute)

No one knows your story
Nobody cares to know your truth.
Behind your eyes and in your heart
There's the remnants of abuse.
The times you felt less than nothing
And when the world told you the same
Who was there to wipe your tears?
Who said it would be okay?

The pain stems from your childhood
In the home you thought was safe
Who was there to protect you?
When your daddy went away.
When the teachers had no confidence
They thought you'd never finish school
When you struggled with your work
They made you feel you were a fool.

There was no one to look up to
For you to aspire and want to be
Because the women all around you
Were hurting just as badly.
Everyday you've had to fight
Just to get the things you need
When you shout loud enough to be heard
You're accused of doing so angrily.

I know what you've been through
I see you hustle constantly
I recognise the person within you
An angry Black Woman lives inside of me.

For I'm no victim
I won't justify my ways
Being a Black Woman is hard
I remember that each day.
My life has been defined
By other races and many kinds
I've been labelled and judged
By the Angry Black Woman stereotype.
Without even trying
I'm loud, arrogant and strong
My own men don't want me
Because they think I'm doing wrong.

Every corner of the earth
An angry Black Woman resides
It's a label we can't fight
A syndrome that's a lie.
We have the power
To redefine our legacy
We're the mothers of the earth
We birthed humanity.

To recognise our strength
We must know our history.
We're descendants of excellence
We are Princesses and Nubian Queens.
The passion that we hold
Could be used constructively.

We've no need to be angry
Just to find our self-esteem.
For those who don't like us
That is of no concern
Until we see the good in us
We have a lot to learn.

The grass isn't always greener: Shattering an illusion

Sharmaine lived around the corner from me. We had played on the local streets together as children. My sister and I didn't know very much about Sharmaine except for the fact she was very light skinned in comparison to her family members. We later discovered that Sharmaine's father was mixed raced.

'I can't believe you're less than a year older than me! I said to Sharmaine one Saturday evening (in 2008) on a bus ride home from work. She had beckoned for me to come and sit beside her on the back seat. We got talking and I learnt more about her in 20 minutes than I had done in two decades.

'All those years you played outside on your own. You seemed so grown up'. That was my way of being polite. I really wanted to ask Sharmaine why her parents allowed her to be on the streets by herself at such a young age.

Sharmaine's sister Shanika was the neighbourhood bully and more than a decade older than us. She was, tall and slender with a constantly angry face expression. Shanika was a tyrant who was really mean to my sister and I. She always referred to us as the 'trampy Africans'. As a child I couldn't connect the sisters. They bore no physical similarities. Sharmaine was chubby, short and had a cute smiley face. She was always nice to us, irritatingly kind. In fact there were times when we would try and avoid her.

'You never saw us together. Ever!' Sharmaine reiterated about the status of her relationship with Shanika 'Not even when we were younger. We still don't get on'. Sharmaine took a sip from the tin of beer. We had alighted from the bus 10 minutes before and were sitting on a bench outside our local off licence.

'She has always been jealous of me' Sharmaine added. Her hazel brown eyes were watering. I wasn't sure whether it was caused by the whistling breeze or the fact that she was overwhelmed by the story she was about to tell me.

Sharmaine's life had been tough. At the time of our conversation Sharmaine was living in a hostel and was estranged from her immediate family. Over the years I would recall that there were periods where we wouldn't see her in the neighbourhood for months at a time because she would relocate to another town. We were sitting on a bench where the local low life's congregated as Sharmaine slurped from a large can of extra strong beer. I was curious to know why she believed that Shanika envied her. By

122

no means was her life perfect but Shanika worked full time, owned a flat and a small car. Shanika had a beautiful teenage son and had maintained a close relationship to their mother, the type of relationship which Sharmaine pined for. Why would she be jealous of Sharmaine?

'My family think my life should be easier because I'm light skinned' she muttered.

'Oh really' I said nonchalantly.

'Yep' Sharmaine went onto explain why. 'I take after my dad w she point towards the freckles that were scatters across the bridge of her nose.

'Who is your dad?' I thought he might be someone I'd seen in the area without realising the connection.

'You will never see him!. I've got a picture of him. He looks kind of Arab. I haven't seen him in years'. Sharmaine's family instilled the belief that her life should be smooth sailing because she had a lighter complexion. They were all very dark skinned. This had given Sharmaine an inferiority complex and put a great deal of pressure on her to succeed. This may have been the reason why (at 24 years old) she was a heavy drinker and very depressed. She hadn't finished school or managed to pursue a tangible career. Her family hadn't taught her that life is what you make it. Hard work, self-respect and stability sets the foundation for anything you wish to pursue! This sista was suffering because of family's misconception about complexion. Perhaps they were all jealous and resented her which is the reason that she seemed to have been neglected.

Sharmaine saw her race as a hindrance. Unfortunately it hadn't afforded her the so called privileges that her family spoke of or anticipated would be thrown at her because of her mixed heritage.

'My granddad was very dark skinned, he was a Maroon. I think dark skinned people are pretty. I wish I was born African' Sharmaine said. This statement was ironic. When we were growing up in Lewisham there weren't many West Indian children would have expressed their desire to be African. Certainly not in those days. Yet Sharmaine seemed to believe that her life would have been entirely different if this was the case. I was saddened by her stories of bereavement, sexual abuse and depression. She was clearly suicidal. Her problems had very little to do with her complexion. From what I could gather it was the fact that her family hardly seemed to have any time for her. She needed love, attention and to be nurtured. She craved for motherly love. By the sounds of it her mother had been too emotionally hurt to give it to her. As the aged old saying goes, hurt people hurt people.

'My mum said she didn't want any more kids after Shanika'. This statement was problematic in itself. Why did anyone need to tell her that her mother didn't necessarily want her? What was the point, even if it was the truth?

'My uncle said he's surprised that I'm still alive' Sharmaine was shaking her head. This wasn't a suitable announcement to make to a young person? I appreciate that she was quite a troublesome girl but why was everything so negative. This type of comment made Sharmaine feel very unwanted. I recall as child that I never saw her accompanied by an adult. NEVER!

Sharmaine also told me that she was being visited by the spirit of her grandmother who died almost 20 years before, it was clear that she was at her lowest point. Her father was absent, mother a workaholic and her sister plagued by jealousy. It's no surprise that Sharmaine felt the way she did.

A year after this conversation my brother had informed me that Sharmaine had been sent to prison. My encounter with her that day had prompted me to think about complexion from a light skinned perspective. Not everything that glitters is gold. Sharmaine's path had defied the widely shared belief amongst Blacks that having light skin equates to an easier life.

Racial Reinstatement

We need to learn our history
To embrace one another.
We must respect ourselves
So we can love each other.

If we don't realise that we form one team.
How can we gather strength?
How will we reach our dreams?
The road has been long
We have fought all the way
But we have to keep going
To see a better day.

Our attitude to learning
Is our attitude to living.
To educate ourselves
Is our only chance of winning.

Be proud of who you are
You can't be no one else
If you don't respect yourself
How can somebody else?

Never be ashamed
Be true to where you're coming from
Our ancestors were great
That greatness kept them strong.

Look into the mirror
And think of what you see
There much more to yourself
Then you've been led to believe.

Fill the gap of knowledge
Absorb your history
If you don't find your truth
Then everything's a mystery!

Summary

I revisited the original questions and queries that ignited my desire to write the Melanin Monologues. I appreciate that I have a greater awareness and will be open to acquire more information about the subject of race. Here are the findings that I gathered in my self-exploration of race relations.

When did I become conscious of colour?

Primary school was the very first environment where my formal education about race began. I was socialised with people outside my immediate and extended family network. My peers drew this difference to my attention. I learnt about what it meant to be Black and African. Sure enough there were Black children in my school, many of them originated from the West Indies, South America and Southern Asia. Blackness had subcategories and proved itself to be very divisive. There were Black people who were light skinned and those who were dark. Then there were Caribbean Black folks and the Africans. There were those who had coolie hair (Black and Indian ancestry) and people like me whose hair was course and kinky. These were categories that were not historically invented by Black people (the slave masters can take credit for this) but are enforced and maintained by us in present day. These parameters were so important to our sense of being and value. For the less African (Sub Saharan) you looked the prettier and more intelligent you were and it was thought that the greater chance you had of being successful in life. My colour was negatively defined in this space and I was fully aware of how my dark complexion and African heritage made me different to the other Black children.

What does being Black mean to me?

Strangely enough being Black means everything and nothing to me at the same time. I think about my colour and complexion quite a lot, virtually every single day which I believe is a lot more than people who are light skinned and white tend do. I am reminded of my complexion due to its difference to those who appear in the media and

127

in everyday life, where whiteness and/or having light skin is deemed as the norm. Take a look at the advertisements. The majority of people who model and feature in these areas (as they promote everyday products) have lighter skin. When I purchase magazines and there are samples of foundation makeup products inside, more often than not the shade isn't suitable for very dark (Black) complexions. This may sound very petty but ask a handful of dark skinned people the same question and the majority (especially women who live in western societies) are likely to share the same view.

I factor in the importance of being Black when I apply for jobs and when I'm visiting areas outside of multi-cultural districts. When I say 'factor' I mean that there is a need for me to consider and evaluate how my race can potentially be a negative or positive aspect of the experience. For example when visiting regions where there are no other people of colour, as a dark skinned person you constantly get stared at which isn't so bad. It's when you receive a hostile response in form of a racist comment or another statement which lets you know that your presence isn't welcomed in that environment. Ask any Black person with common sense and who has been socially conditioned. Nine times out of ten they will express a very similar if not identical view. In this instance it's about preserving personal safety. If you don't have your instinct attuned to this aspect of subliminal social coding it could have detrimental effects. If this statement is upsetting for you to read then that's regrettable as it wasn't meant to cause any offence, but ITS THE TRUTH and a reoccurring reality for a large percentage of people of colour.

When I refer to the point that 'Blackness means nothing to me', it stems from an element of frustration. As a Black person there are certain aspects of our African and Caribbean culture that has been practiced for thousands of years. Take for instance dance, music, fashion and beauty. In addition to popular inventions such as well as Dr Charles Drew (Blood Bank), Thomas L Jenkins (Dry Cleaning process), Garrett Augustus Morgan (the gas mask and first traffic light signal) and George Washington Carver (agricultural chemist). Perhaps you weren't aware that these were invented by people of African descent? Once these things became mainstream and commercialised they were disassociated from its Black influence and no longer acknowledged as its source of creation. Unless you have been educated about how the trend or product was developed. In turn other races become better at operating and engaging in the things that were once affiliated with Black culture, more so than Black people themselves. The positive thing about this type of exposure is that it brings elements of our culture to people who otherwise wouldn't have known it existed. But it must have been frustrating for the innovators and their descendants.

The same can be said in reference to the entertainment industry. The soaring records sales and popularity of the pretty blonde Australian artist Iggy Azealea can be regarded as her ability to be rapping, dancing, wearing cornrows and speaking in slang and having a bigger booty than a Black female artist. Her image is influenced by elements that were originally cultivated by Black hip-hop artists. This might sound quite trivial but it's the truth. A white lady takes stereotypical bits of Black peoples characteristics, behavioural traits and culture. The artist goes onto sell millions of records. In this case I find it quite bizarre. How on earth can she sound like that, she's from Australia not an American ghetto? This is relatively inauthentic. Azealea's case is just one example but the appropriation of Black/African culture happens quite frequently.

Why am I alienated because of my skin colour?

Everywhere there are people of colour whether they be Black, Asian, mixed raced, Native Indian, Aboriginal or any other background, a colour coded cast system exists. The more European one looks, the more beautiful one is deemed and the higher your potential social status. This trend isn't new, it's no secret, it's not accidental, it's a way of life. As long as you're a person of colour regardless of where you live in this world you'll understand and accept this categorisation as a universal belief. The concept is embedded in our psyche and it's a part of our social conditioning which means it's readily enforced as we grow up and integrate with others.

Blackness, particularly in Africa and Australia was redefined by Europeans who infiltrated these regions and influenced the indigenous people's perception of self. Their traditional cultural practices were subdued and standardised as the Europeans took ownership of their lands and the rule of governing the original inhabitants.

Their ideals of beauty, politics and other aspects of European traditions and societal systems where supplemented in place of the indigenous people's own. As Black people we know that we were enslaved, indoctrinated and transported to western shores to work as part of a labour force. Historically this level of Eurocentric conditioning remained imprinted in our brains and passed onto later generations. The treatment that Black people encountered from our captors became our template for how we socialised with one another and the way that we reared later generations.

I understand that my perception and the definition of Black in a westernized context is historically enforced. Europeans were the rulers of wealth and power. On the other hand Blackness was and continues to be fashioned in terms of its difference to whiteness. Therefore the concepts are binary oppositions. If Blackness is bad then whiteness is good. If poverty exists in close proximity to being Black then wealth and prosperity is encapsulated by being white. If white is pretty then you can be sure that being ugly is affiliated with Blackness. You see everything that whiteness is, blackness is not. In turn with the application of this logic my Blackness is alienated because it's the furthest thing from whiteness. I can never be white or embody the things that the concept of whiteness brings (purity, morality). I think there are a substantial amount of Black people who don't necessarily want to be white. They want to have unlimited access to the advantages that the world believes whiteness brings, accommodates and achieves. Nevertheless if you're Black then social structures, beliefs systems as well as basic definitions of the words (Black and white) ensure this isn't possible.

How and when did this inferiority complex begin?

Although I use the term inferiority I don't consciously feel that I have been entrapped by being a Black person. I speak of the subconscious societal practices, conditioning and behaviour that relegates Black people to a lower social status.

For example if we examine the socio-political terms that have been used to identify people of colour in the UK and USA. Particularly the phrase ethnic minority. Examine the parent word for minority, the term minor. To be minor means that one is under age and yet to have full legal responsibility of themselves. Basically it refers to being in a childlike state. If one is a minor they are regarded as being insignificant or lacking any position of importance in the areas of which they occupy. Please check your dictionary (a comprehensive one) and explore the meaning in its truest form. To be a minority in this capacity demonstrates ones inferiority to the dominant racial group. Recognising this suggests how fundamental it becomes for us to be conscious of what people call us and how we choose to embrace or reject such labels. These are damaging to our self-esteem and our potential to empower ourselves as we are taught that we are a minority. Minors are not seen to be mature enough to make their own decisions nor can they have the power to contribute to the remits of other groups or movements. Is there any society or space in the wealthy western world where minors are decision makers? Or form part of the power structure?

I became aware of my inferiority complex when I understood how Black people were labelled. Subsequently I knew that the so called complex wasn't organic to my existence it was actually imposed upon me and my peers. How? The point is that people of colour don't have the resources and/or power to construct social-political terms that are used by governments to identify our racial classifications. We don't occupy the professional positions which enforce these concepts and ideals.

In the past we condemned the use of the term Nigger. I mean the word Nigger as it was used politically, formally and interchanging when referring to a Negro. Not the word Nigga (Never Ignorant Getting Goals Accomplished- Tupac Shakur) that continues to be used in films, music and other aspects of popular contemporary culture.

As a community who campaigned for our civil rights and embraced the Black power movement, the government's move towards political correctness led to the abandonment of the words Nigger and Negro. Ultimately regardless of how much pressure the Black community put on the government to cease the use of these two N words, let's ask ourselves whose decision counts in the reinvention of any terminology used to identify Black folks and people of colour? Well there goes your answer. If you're Black and you don't necessarily feel inferior in a wider context beyond the community and country you inhabit there are greater forces who have secured your minority and inferior state of being. Observe the pattern of beliefs and values in your environment. When these are widely disseminated amongst the majority of people it becomes a shared consensus amongst the dominant group which is thought of as the truth. In reality or in its original sense it may well have been the opposite.

There was a time up until the 1960s when Black people were fighting for their civil rights. Civility in terms of law is concerned with ordinary citizens, once again I ask that you check your dictionaries for the meanings of civil law and civil rights. Think about equality and human rights for every day citizens like yourself, your family, neighbourhoods, colleagues and so forth. These are basic rights that Black people had to fight for like voting, housing, employment, good education even riding certain buses to get to work. Of course you would recognise your inferior status if you had to campaign for the right to have access to resources that other races had in abundance and could take for granted. How could you not be thought of as inferior if there were groups in society who argued and denied you of these things on the basis of race and not because of anything in particular you had or hadn't done?

For me inferiority relates to how Blackness is defined and perceived by other communities outside of the Black race, particularly the white ruling elite classes in western societies. In reality it doesn't matter what I or other Black people think about our heritage because we don't dictate how we are perceived in the media. In turn these images of us are projected and broadcast to audiences across the globe, many of whom don't get the opportunity to interact with people of colour in their everyday lives. Understandably they grasp their view of Black culture and history from what they see on TV. These portrayals haven't necessarily been filtered by the media network's in favour of positively presenting Blacks. More often than not the depictions reinforce the negative stereotypes. Who can challenge these portrayals if they don't have any other imagery which counteracts these views. There is very little to compare it with.

The schooling system that I was a part of ignited the perpetual view of Blackness as an inferior state of being. A disproportionally large amount of Black pupils had special educational needs, their attainment grades were below the national average expected for their age and the majority of exclusions from school were Black male pupils.

The concept of being inferior was triggered by being bombarded with negative images of Africans in books and documentaries. Every time we addressed African culture (with the exception of Ancient Egypt) at school the theme was always the same. I was taught about famine, poverty, Aids, sickness, malaria, cholera and contaminated water. I learnt about Bob Geldof's mission to alleviate Ethiopia from drought and starvation. The school syllabus and teaching staff didn't ever address or highlight African wealth such as natural resources (oil, gas, water, minerals, diamond, coal, rubber, titanium. The list goes on and on. I wasn't encouraged to learn about the great empires of Mali, Ghana and Benin in West Africa and their specialism in trading, carpentry and making Bronze statues and tools. I was told nothing about this! Nada, Zilch. I didn't hear about the Moors of North Western Africa and how they influenced the architecture of the castles that still stand in Europe today. The first I heard about the Moors was in the tale of Othello that gave me a slight taste of the Black influence on literature and Africans relationship with the European population, from a white perspective.

Why I needed to learn about my Blackness and reconnect with it?

If you are told something about yourself for long enough especially when you are young and impressionable, you start to believe it. My peers, teachers and many aspects of the media have shown me that I'm not good enough to achieve anything worthwhile or having anything of great value in this society. These judgements weren't necessarily based on the merit of my academic achievements or my personality. There is evidence to suggest that they were formed on the basis of my skin. How? There were so few Black skinned women in influential positions. With the exception of the wonderful Oprah Winfrey. But as a Black girl from South-East London I needed to see someone closer to home flying the flag of success for dark skinned Black people.

You eventually get fed up of being at the bottom and always having to explain yourself. Why you have certain cultural practices, what your name means or why you wear your hair in such intricate hairstyles. I felt like I was an excuse, a sorry one at that. My skin and hair weren't celebrated in mainstream culture so I've had to find places were my Blackness is holistically embraced. Black people have been a part of British society for centuries. Even before the influx of immigration from African and the West Indies in the late 1940s post World War Two. We were here in the UK as students in the 1880s, there were Black people in Britain before then.

If you're a UK based person reading this you maybe defensive or disagree with what I am saying and that's fine. Ask yourself this? When was the last time you saw a very dark skinned person on TV? I'm not talking about a person who is acting, singing, playing sports or making jokes? I'm suggesting you try and spot a dark skinned Black African looking person advertising a popular brand of shampoo or a popular moisturising cream. It may well happen but not often enough for us to readily remember.

I needed to reconnect with my Blackness so that I don't forget, resent or reject it. If images of Black women are largely missing from the realm of the public spotlight then it's my responsibility to search for it in other places in order to find that sense of positive reinforcement. As Black people we can no longer turn to other races for validation of our beauty and self-worth.

In the past I've tried to hide the things about my heritage that are quintessentially African like my hair. I have been chemically straightening my hair since the age of 12 and wearing hair extensions for as long as I can remember. For a short while I'd forgotten what my natural hair looked like. Then I began to wonder what my hair behaved like in its natural state. Why had I been hiding it? Sure my hair is nappy and short but it's the hair that I was born with. My ancestors who I claimed to be so proud of had the very same hair. Then there was my skin colour. It's darker than most of the people around me. What significance is that? If those who are light skinned, brown skinned and white can wear their skin with pride then why can't I? Finally I saw the need to love my complexion the way other people take pride in their own. My skin is very dark and I'm extremely proud. It is beautiful because it's indicative of my country of origin and ancestral lineage dating back thousands of years. My dark skin is brilliant because it serves it biological purpose when the sun is beaming down on the world. No matter what the media says or shows or what the big screen portrays. I don't care if there isn't a single dark face on TV. Black isn't just Beautiful, it's magnificent. There are times when I think that other races are more aware of this than Black people themselves, irrespective of what they may say in the public eye.

I urge dark skinned people to engage with your Blackness if you want to elevate your sense of being as well as uphold your self-worth and self-esteem. If you want to achieve something great in this life then you have to accept and love yourself first and foremost. How can you strive for brilliance if you have no value? Subconsciously you will feel that you aren't worthy of good things.

I've learnt that there isn't any point in being ashamed of who you are. You will never get respect for trying to be something that you're not. Fair enough, if you want to bleach your skin then that's your prerogative but others can tell that your newly acquired complexion is artificial. How would anybody take you seriously for aspiring to be something that you can never achieve naturally? In doing show you are reinforcing self-hatred.

Why is it important to identify with my Blackness in a westernised society?

Being a Black person takes a great deal of effort. There are times when very dark skinned people's needs aren't catered to in mainstream and popular culture.

When I've needed simple things like makeup and hair care products I can't just walk into any high street cosmetics store or supermarket to purchase the products that most other women can acquire at the drop of a hat. There are times when I have to make do with what's available by mixing and blending merchandise for the most suitable results. The same can be said for the preparation and cooking of foods from my country of origin. The supermarkets in multicultural cities have made great improvements in stocking these items, some now have 'ethnic' and 'world food' aisles.

As a Black person we are deemed to be different in westernised societies and are taught that we exist outside the societal norms. There are instances where this means with have to constantly explain our culture. Not everyone needs to be aware of our cultural practices because it exists outside of the dominant view.

This is why I say that if you want to learn more about being Black and your ancestral origins it takes a great deal of effort. Your children might not be given the opportunity to learn very much about Black History at school. African history will not take precedence over European history in the syllabus of many schools. The system will fulfil the academic needs of the white majority first and foremost.

You will have to visit Africa, bookshops, surf the internet and watch documentaries in your spare time to enlighten yourself. Unfortunately for African people great Black history hasn't been sign posted nor will it be placed beneath our noses. Research is necessary to educate yourself about yourself.

I guess that this relates to what Cress Welsing (1991) says about educating ourselves about racism otherwise we risk being stuck in an ignorant state, which in effect can be damaging to our progress as people particularly if we don't operate as an entire unit moving in the same direction.

Conclusion

Being a dark skinned person is a big responsibility, one that I take very seriously. I'm a self-appointed ambassador for dark skinned people. Why? When I was growing up it was so important for me to see people who looked like me doing positive things because they were a reflection of me. If they could achieve something then I knew I could do the same. I recognise that I could potentially inspire others (regardless of their skin tone) in much the same way. I am required to remind myself that my choices and subsequent decisions influence others. I strongly believe in the age old saying that we should become the change that we want to see in the world. So here I am with a chronicle of my perception of a subject very close to my heart.

Learning about my heritage is vital because knowledge of Black history wasn't readily available to me in the classroom. At school I was taught very little about the achievements of Black people outside the context of slavery. These are important things for Black people to know in order to build our self-esteem. We had a history before we came into contact with the Europeans and were transported to other corners of the world. Black people have such a strong culture and ruled empires. We were traders, scholars, royalty, architects and amongst other great professions. As Black Africans we practice all of the prestigious professions that exist in modern day society. Many of the strategies and methods that are popular duties carried out in many of these roles originated in Africa. They were learnt by European travellers who came into Africa who adapted and brought the teachings and skill set back to western societies.

There were great civilizations and kingdoms operating across Africa. Many that co-existed with the Ancient Egyptian Empire. The Kingdom of Axum, The Kingdom of Ghana, the Mali Empire, the Songhai Empire to name a few. How would we ever know these things if we aren't told about them? Evidently we are responsible for our own personal development and must seek the information to fill in the gaps in our knowledge. I promise the facts, truth and details are out there. How will we know unless we go looking for it?

Writing the monologues has awakened my spirit and opened up my eyes. I've removed my rose tinted glasses and expanded my mind in order to see things for how they really are. I've come to accept that I was very impressionable regardless of how strong I thought I was. Race has greatly influenced my entire life, including the way I view myself. I fully understand the responsibility that I have as an individual who belongs to a race of people who have had such a tumultuous past wherever they have resided.

I feel empowered because I know more about my ancestors and that has inspired my determination to reach my aspired destination.

I want to reiterate that the monologues is a Black British perspective. This is my story whether people choose to like it or not. As I've said I'm not trying to offend anyone. I'm simply speaking my own truth. A love and appreciation for my dark skin, my fellow Black people and African culture doesn't equate to my resenting any other race. I am placing myself at the forefront of this project and my lifelong agenda because I've been exposed to cultures and systems of belief for as long as I can remember. I can respectfully say that there is room for people to learn about other people's heritage. In fact that's quite healthy especially if you live in a multicultural environment. Cultural awareness gives us a greater capacity for understanding the people who are our neighbours.

Documenting my past encounters of race in chronological order was very therapeutic. I felt a sense of closure. It triggered my memory of incidents that had laid dominant in my mind for a number of years. The monologues has been a mind mapping exercise which has enabled me to express myself without restraint. After reflecting upon a few past situations that made me angry, I've found that I can make peace with myself and move on with my life.

As I was writing up this conclusion my brother and I sat in a fast food restaurant discussing our latest projects.

'After I've finished writing the Melanin Monologues I'm going to put this whole skin complexion debate to bed. I'm not talking about it anymore!' I said as I nibbled at my fries.

'Why?' he frowned.

'I'm tired. I've spent so many years thinking and talking about being dark skinned. I'm just fed up'. The truth is my complexion became an obsession. To be totally oblivious of it would be unrealistic. My skin dictates how the world sees me. Our skin is the most distinctive difference between us as human beings. However I have spent my entire life defending my skin colour. Now I want to enjoy other areas of life that have been clouded by my preoccupation with the belief that there are certain things I can't do because I'm Black. Or for the fact that no other Black person has achieved it before . You see sometimes we fail because we don't try.

I tell people of colour as I remind myself. Try to pursue the things that you believe in and that you consider can contribute positively to your future. Your colour can be as much of an obstacle as you choose to make it. We can achieve at times of adversity! We need self-belief and motivation. Yes, inequality and injustice do exist, its prevalence means that we have to work that extra bit harder. But it's worth it.

That day as I sat at the restaurant, my brother was sceptical of my declaration to abandon the skin complexion debate. Maybe I don't need to, it could be my duty to spread the word and bring the issue to the forefront of people's attention. I know it makes people feel uncomfortable, but so what. There other day I was at work and I was taking to a colleague about the way people criticised me for having dark skin when I was a child. I wanted to test out his reaction. After five minutes he went very red and remained silent.

'I suppose there are all sorts of discrimination out there' he stuttered 'if you're poor, if you're Black, if you're disabled, if you're gay' he added and I knew this was my cue to change the subject before he exploded. His skin was getting brighter by the second. If he felt uncomfortable then how did he imagine I felt?

In writing these monologues my objective had been to complete a project that provided a Black British female perspective of race and racism. The British dimension is an important contribution to the existing and expansive library of racial dialogue. African American's literature on race is relatively large in comparison. Black UK based people represent a smaller community yet we have so many great stories to bring to the table for the benefit of a global understanding of the Black experience in contemporary society.

I'm not a psychiatrist or psychologist and it wasn't my aim to prove or disprove existing academic theories. The Melanin Monologues is an oral testimony. There are books, documentaries and other research materials that provide in depth discussions about race, identity, melanin you name it. If you're interested to learn more go out there and tap into this information. You will be able to draw your own conclusions from what you see and read.

Perhaps there will be a Melanin Monologues 2 which will align its self with my original aim to compile the stories of people who feel strongly about the impact race has had upon their lives and how it continues to influence the direction they choose to take in life. I should think that the monologues will inspire people of all races to publish their own accounts. If so that would be great. Even if you are the only person reading this book then my mission has truly been accomplished. As long as it has encouraged you to think more positively about your own racial identity and to closely examine any information that is placed in front of you. Remember anything worth having is not likely to be accessible for all. The same came be said about the recordings of Black history. You will have to dig a little deeper to find the good stuff.

In any case if the Melanin Monologues stimulates your thinking and uplifts you enough to feel the need to do all the above. Then I've already achieved my goal.

References

Biko, S (1978) I Write What I Like: Steven Biko. A Selection of his Writings (ed.) Stubbs, A (fl.1978). Oxford. Heinemann 1987.

Channsin, D. & Duke, B. (2013) Dark Girls. Documentary. Image Entertainment.

Dovi, Efam (2007) Bringing water to Africa's poor: African Renewal Online (www.un.org/africarenewal/magazine/october-2007/bringing-water-africa%E2%80%99s-poor website accessed 2nd September 2014

Henry, W. L. (2007) Whiteness Made Simple: Stepping into the Grey Zone. London: Nu-Beyond Limited: Learning by Choice.

King, Richard (1994) Melanin: A Key to Freedom, with an extensive glossary and bibliography. USA: MD U.B & U.S Communication Systems

Knox, Robert (1850) The Races of Men: A Fragment. Nabu Press.

Oxford dictionary (2008) Eleventh Edition. Oxford University Press Inc., New York.

Welsing, F. C. (1991) The Isis Paper: The Keys to the Colors. Chicago: Third World Press.

Windsor, R. R (1988) From Babylon to Timbuktu: A History of Ancient Black Races Including the Black Hebrews. New York: Exposition Press Inc.

Other sources

Ora, Rita (2014) Interview on The Breakfast Club, 105.1 FM. 23rd April 2014, New York. USA

Printed in Great Britain
by Amazon.co.uk, Ltd.,
Marston Gate.